William Sha

Measure for

In a new version by Josie Rourke

methuen | drama
LONDON · NEW YORK · OXFORD · NEW DELHI · SYDNEY

METHUEN DRAMA
Bloomsbury Publishing Plc
50 Bedford Square, London, WC1B 3DP, UK
1385 Broadway, New York, NY 10018, USA

BLOOMSBURY, METHUEN DRAMA and the Methuen Drama logo are
trademarks of Bloomsbury Publishing Plc

This edition first published 2018

A catalogue record for this book is available from the British Library.

A catalog record for this book is available from the Library of Congress.

ISBN: PB: 978-1-350-10205-7
ePDF: 978-1-350-10207-1
eBook: 978-1-350-10206-4

Series: Modern Plays

Typeset by Mark Heslington Ltd, Scarborough, North Yorkshire
Printed and bound in Great Britain

To find out more about our authors and books visit
www.bloomsbury.com and sign up for our *newsletters*.

CAST *(in order of speaking)*

Duke Vincentio	**Nicholas Burns**
Escalus	**Raad Rawi**
Angelo	**Jack Lowden**
Thomas	**Anwar Russell**
Mistress Overdone	**Rachel Denning**
Lucio	**Matt Bardock**
Pompey	**Jackie Clune**
Claudio	**Sule Rimi**
Provost	**Adam McNamara**
Isabel	**Hayley Atwell**
Francisca	**Molly Harris**
Mariana/Justice	**Helena Wilson**
Frederick/Justice	**Ben Allen**

PRODUCTION

Director   Josie Rourke
Designer   Peter McKintosh
Lighting Designer   Howard Harrison
Sound Designer   Emma Laxton
Composer   Michael Bruce
Casting Director   Alastair Coomer CDG

Introduction: An Unromantic Comedy

During the 1590s, Shakespeare developed his own distinctive version of the romcom: typically set in a distant or fairy-tale location – like Illyria, or the Forest of Arden – where disguise and confusion enable a prominent female character to pursue her own marriage choice, independent of patriarchal authority and flanked by some minor couples who also get hitched at the end of the play, with a bit of musical hey-nonny-nonny to add to the general merriment. It's familiar stuff. First printed in 1623 amid these plays under the heading of 'Comedies', *Measure for Measure* both is, and is not, a comedy. It comes later than *A Midsummer Night's Dream*, *Much Ado About Nothing* and *Twelfth Night*, as London settled to the reign of the new king James I and Shakespeare's acting company took on the honorific title of the King's Men. Its take on romantic comedy is mordantly provocative. Here our determined heroine, Isabella, is set against, rather than towards, marriage; the setting is grimly urban rather than escapistly pastoral; and a repressive patriarchy is firmly in charge. Whereas previous Shakespearean comedies sublimated sexual desire into erotically charged wordplay, and left its couples decorously at the bedroom door, *Measure for Measure* depicts sex before, outside and instead of marriage. It is a distinctly, and deliberately, unromantic comedy.

What makes this twist on the generic template so unsettling is that we can still see the perverse outlines of rejected romantic comedy within the play. It is, for example, deeply uncomfortable to acknowledge both that Isabella's two interviews with Angelo are framed by inequality and coercion, and/but they also crackle with suppressed sexual connection. Shakespeare writes these scenes in the style of courtship scenes – think Beatrice and Benedick, or Rosalind and Orlando – where lovers pay heightened attention to each other, swapping lines and rhythms and imagery in powerfully intimate interlocking speeches. But the content here belies those associations, because this is not wooing, but enforced, unmutual sexual domination and bullying. There are other examples of romantic comedy gone bad, twisted into darker, more sinister shapes. The Duke's friar costume mimics those benign comic disguises that enable truth-telling and dramatic resolution; here it is freighted with unaccountability and the callous abuse of power. When, at the end of the play, we see the multiple marriages with which comedies typically conclude, these do not here symbolise social regeneration and renewal. Rather they are compelled couplings that represent commuted punishments for men, and that seem indifferent to the fate of the women. There is no real reason for optimism at the end of *Measure for Measure*, since none of the personal, social and sexual dysfunction which prompted the drama of the Duke's abdication has been resolved.

Perhaps the play's most significant swerve from the values of Shakespearean romantic comedy comes in its attitudes to women. Whereas previously female desire constructed the genre, as comic heroines go get their man, here in *Measure for Measure* desire is dangerously, violently masculine. Apart from Claudio's pregnant girlfriend Juliet, who defends him against the unspoken crime of non-consensual sex, none of the play's women seems able to participate as an equal. The unseen, offstage prostitutes who work in Mistress Overdone's brothel somehow symbolise a larger exclusion of women as proper autonomous agents in the play. Isabella does not want to have sex with Angelo, or with anyone: she has committed herself at the beginning of the play to the life of the convent. No one in Vienna – not Angelo, certainly, but not her brother Claudio, or Lucio, or the Duke, and perhaps not even the theatre audience – is willing to allow her that choice. Modern critics have not tended to like Isabella much, and have thus been surprisingly ambivalent about her conduct, arguing, Angelo-like, over various Renaissance theologies of sexuality that would apparently excuse her capitulation to the deputy's monstrous proposition. It is often implied, both in the play and beyond it, that she is somehow cold or priggish in placing her own bodily autonomy over that of her brother. In the end, Isabella's rights to her own body can only be temporarily secured by sacrificing another woman, Mariana, to Angelo's desires. Isabella loses dramatic agency at this point: having been articulate and outspoken, she is increasingly silenced by the Duke's hectic plotting. The play is ruthless in dividing female solidarity: women are forced into collusion with male authority. Isabella, it seems, can never return to the sisterhood of St Clare's: she is plucked from the convent into a fallen world in which the Duke's unanswered marriage proposal is, like the marriages of Angelo and Mariana, and of Lucio and the absent Kate Keepdown, a kind of punishment.

In that final scene, it seems that the Duke is the only character on stage still valiantly committed to the implausible idea that he is directing a romantic comedy. In trying to bring about marriages among his unwilling subjects, the Duke attempts to tidy transgressive urges into a socially and generically acceptable shape, to redirect dangerous desire into respectable marriages, to turn the dark sexuality of a Vienna we might associate with its famous later resident Sigmund Freud into the wholesome romances of Arden. His exertions in the long final scene are exhausting as he works to create comedy from the human wreckage around him. Perhaps this is Shakespeare's retrospective reflection on the ultimate never-never land of romantic comedy. Perhaps it registers the pragmatic influence of the city playwright Thomas Middleton, who probably revised Shakespeare's play, dirtying it up for London audiences tiring of Arcadian lovers and girls dressed as boys, and with an appetite for grittier scenarios and more compromised conclusions. Either way, it makes for a play which generates urgently contemporary questions about sex, power and society. As we assess the ongoing impact of #MeToo revelations on our relationships, behaviours and institutions, there is no more pressing and relevant Shakespearean play than *Measure for Measure*.

Emma Smith
Hertford College, Oxford

Measure for Measure

Characters *(in order of speaking)*

Duke Vincentio, *the Duke of Vienna*
Escalus, *a judge in Vienna*
Angelo, *a young man, the Duke's deputy in Vienna (Part One); a young man entering a religious retreat (Part Two)*
Thomas, *a friar (Part One); a retreat member (Part Two)*
Mistress Overdone, *a madam*
Lucio, *a lawyer*
Pompey, *a pimp*
Justice, *an officer of the court*
Claudio, *Isabel's brother (Part One); Angelo's brother (Part Two)*
Provost, *an officer of the court*
Isabel, *a young woman entering a religious retreat (Part One); a young woman, the Duke's deputy in Vienna (Part Two)*
Francisca, *a nun (Part One); a retreat member (Part Two)*
Mariana, *Angelo's former fiancée (Part One)*
Frederick, *Isabel's former fiancé (Part Two)*

A Note on the Text

This version of *Measure for Measure* is cut down from the original and fashioned into two parts of equal length, each of five acts. They are almost identical, except for one significant change: the gender of the novice and the deputy reverses in each version.

In many respects, Part One plays as first published. The original plot of a male deputy (Angelo) propositioning the female novice (Isabella) in an exchange for her brother's life is unchanged. In Part Two, the genders of deputy and novice reverse. The deputy is played by the female actor who was the novice, and the novice is played by the male actor who was the deputy. In both Parts One and Two, they retain the names 'Angelo' and 'Isabella'.

Although I have not modernised either part of the text, it is imagined that Part One plays in the year it is believed to have been written, 1604, and Part Two plays in the present, 2018.

Act Five of Part One ends with the Duke's marriage proposal to Isabella. It is then intended that Isabella remain onstage and transform from novice nun to the Duke's deputy. Part Two begins with Isabella the Deputy answering the Duke's summons in Act One, Scene One. It is envisaged that the interval comes at the end of Part Two, Act One, Scene One.

In Part Two, Isabella's jilted fiancé is Frederick, rather than Mariana. In the published play, Frederick is Mariana's brother, who is mentioned but does not appear. This means that the fiancé(s) of Angelo and Isabella remain of the opposite gender. However, the Duke's sexuality flips (or expands), as he proposes marriage to Angelo in Part Two, Act Five.

Other than the central gender conceit, it is envisaged that Pompey be played by a woman in both parts, making Mistress Overdone and Pompey a female double act. In Part One, the actor who will play Frederick in Part Two doubles with Justice, and in Part Two, the actor who will play Mariana takes on the Justice role.

In order to reduce the length of the play, I have made some internal cuts and cut some scenes in Mistress Overdone's brothel-house, and in the prison. The main part of the original plot that has been excised is the Duke's attempt to avoid Claudio's execution by finding and temporarily substituting the severed head of another prisoner. In this version, the Duke simply asks that the Provost ignore the execution warrant and conceal Claudio, and the deputy does not request to see his severed head as proof of execution.

Josie Rourke, May 2018

Part One

Act One

Scene One: The Courtroom

Duke, **Escalus** *and* **Provost**.

Duke
Escalus.

Escalus
My lord.

Duke
Of government the properties to unfold
Would seem in me t'affect speech and discourse.
Our city's institutions, and the terms
For common justice, you're as pregnant in
As art and practise hath enriched any
That we remember. There is our commission,
From which we would not have you warp. Call hither,
I say, bid come before us Angelo.
What figure of us think you he will bear?
For you must know we have with special soul
Elected him our absence to supply.

Escalus
If any in Vienna be of worth
To undergo such ample grace and honour,
It is Lord Angelo.

Duke
Look where he comes.

Enter **Angelo**.

Angelo
Always obedient to your grace's will,
I come to know your pleasure.

Duke
Angelo,

There is a kind of character in thy life,
That to the observer doth thy history
Fully unfold. But I do bend my speech
To one that can my part in him advertise;
Hold therefore, Angelo –
In our remove be thou at full ourself;
Mortality and mercy in Vienna
Live in thy tongue and heart: old Escalus,
Though first in question, is thy secondary.
Take thy commission.

Angelo

       Now, good my lord,
Let there be some more test made of my metal,
Before so noble and so great a figure
Be stamp'd upon it.

Duke

       No more evasion:
We have with a leavened and prepared choice
Proceeded to you; therefore take your honours.
Our haste from hence is of so quick condition
That it prefers itself and leaves unquestioned
Matters of needful value. We shall write to you,
How it goes with us. So, fare you well.

Angelo

May we bring you something on the way?

Duke

My haste admits it not. Give me your hand:
I'll privately away. I love the people,
But do not like to stage me to their eyes.
Once more, fare you well.

Escalus

Lead forth and bring you back in happiness!

Duke

I thank you. Fare you well.

Exit **Duke**.

Escalus

    I shall desire you, sir, to give me leave
    To have free speech with you: a power I have,
    But of what strength I am not yet instructed.

Angelo

    'Tis so with me. Let us withdraw together,
    And we may soon our satisfaction have
    Touching that point.

Escalus

                    I'll wait upon your honour.

Exeunt.

Scene Two: The Retreat

Duke *and* **Thomas**.

Duke

    My holy sir, none better knows than you
    How I have ever loved the life removed.
    Why I desire a secret harbour here,
    Hath a purpose.

Thomas

                May your grace speak of it?

Duke

    I have delivered to Judge Angelo,
    My absolute power and place here in Vienna.
    You will demand of me why I do this?

Thomas

    Gladly, my lord.

Duke

    We have strict statutes and most biting laws,
    Which for this fourteen years we have let slip;
    We are more mocked than feared; and our decrees,

Dead to infliction, to themselves are dead;
Thus liberty plucks justice by the nose;
The baby beats the nurse, and quite athwart
Goes all decorum.

Thomas
                It rested in your grace
To unloose this tied-up justice when you pleased:
And it in you more dreadful would have seem'd
Than in Lord Angelo.

Duke
                I do fear, too dreadful:
Sith 'twas my fault to give the people scope,
'Twould be my tyranny to strike and gall them
For what I bid them do. Therefore indeed, my father,
I have on Angelo imposed the office.
I will, as 'twere a member of your order,
Behold his sway. Angelo is precise;
Stands at a guard with envy; scarce confesses
That his blood flows, or that his appetite
Is more to bread than stone: hence shall we see,
If power change purpose, what our seemers be.

Exeunt.

Scene Three: The Courtroom

Justice, **Pompey**, **Mistress Overdone** *and* **Lucio**. **Mistress Overdone** *and* **Pompey** *await trial*. **Lucio** *is defending them*.

Mistress Overdone
I am as well acquainted in this court as I was in our house of profession. One would think it were our own house, for here be many of our old customers.

Lucio
You have not heard of the proclamation, have you?

Mistress Overdone
What proclamation, man?

Lucio

All brothel-houses in the suburbs of Vienna must be
plucked down.

Mistress Overdone

What?

Pompey

To the ground, mistress.

Enter **Escalus** *and* **Angelo**.

Justice

Your honours, these two are accused of keeping a house
of profession, a brothel-house, with many customers.

Escalus

Where were you born?

Pompey

Here in Vienna, sir.

Escalus

What trade are you of in Vienna?

Lucio

She is a tapster, this poor widow's tapster, in her alehouse.
I beseech you, sir, look in this face. Doth your honour
mark this face?

Escalus

Ay, sir, very well.

Lucio

Doth your honour see any harm in this face?

Escalus

Why, no.

Lucio

And her face is the worst thing about her.

Angelo

Your name, mistress?

Mistress Overdone
  Mistress Overdone.

Angelo
  Have you had any more than one husband?

Pompey
  Nine, sir: Overdone by the last.

Angelo
  This will last out a night in Russia
  When nights are longest there. I'll take my leave,
  And leave you to the hearing of the cause,
  Hoping you'll find a good cause to whip them both.

Exit **Angelo**.

Escalus
  Come hither to me, Mistress Tapster. What's your name,
  Mistress Tapster?

Pompey
  Pompey.

Escalus
  What else?

Pompey
  Truly, sir, I am a poor woman that would live.

Escalus
  How would you live, Pompey? By being a bawd? What do
  you think of the trade, Pompey? Is it a lawful trade?

Pompey
  If the law would allow it, sir.

Escalus
  But the law will not allow it, Pompey; nor it shall not be
  allowed in Vienna.

Lucio
  Does your worship mean to geld and splay all the youth of
  the city?

Escalus

No, Lucio.

Lucio

Truly, sir, in my poor opinion, they will to't then. If your worship will take order for the drabs and the knaves, you need not to fear the bawds.

Escalus

There are pretty orders beginning, I can tell you: it is but heading and hanging.

Lucio

If you head and hang all that offend that way, you'll have to give out a commission for more heads: if this law hold in Vienna ten year, I'll rent the fairest house for three-pence a week: if you live to see this come to pass, say I told you so.

Escalus

Thank you, good Lucio; and, in requital of your prophecy, hark you: I advise you, let me not find these two before me again upon any complaint whatsoever; no, not for dwelling where they do: if I do, Lucio, and, in plain dealing, I shall have them both whipped.

Lucio

They thank your worship for your good counsel.

Exit **Escalus** *and* **Justice**. *Enter* **Claudio** *and* **Provost**.

Pompey

Whip me? No, the valiant heart is not whipped out her trade.

Mistress Overdone

Why, here's a change indeed in the commonwealth! What shall become of me?

Pompey

Come; fear you not: good counsellors lack no clients: though you change your place, you need not change your trade. Courage, there will be pity taken on you, you that have almost worked your eyes out in the service. You will be considered.

Mistress Overdone
Well, well; here's one arrested was worth five thousand of us.

Lucio
Who's that?

Mistress Overdone
Claudio.

Lucio
What has he done?

Pompey
A woman.

Lucio
Pray, what's his offence?

Pompey
Groping for trouts in a peculiar river.

Lucio
Why, how now, Claudio! whence comes this restraint?

Mistress Overdone
Let's withdraw.

Exit **Mistress Overdone** *and* **Pompey**.

Claudio
From too much liberty, my Lucio, liberty.

Lucio
What's thy offence, Claudio?

Claudio
What but to speak of would offend again.

Lucio
Is't murder?

Claudio
                    No.

Lucio
                         Lechery?

Claudio
                                   Call it so.
Thus stands it with me: upon a true contract
I got possession of Julietta's bed:
You know the lady; she is fast my wife,
Only for propagation of a dowry
Remaining in the coffer of her friends,
From whom we thought it meet to hide our love
Till time had made them for us. But it chances
The stealth of our most mutual entertainment
With character too gross is writ on Juliet.

Lucio
With child, perhaps?

Claudio
Unhappily, even so. The body public is
A horse whereon this Angelo doth ride,
Who, newly in the seat, that it may know
He can command, lets it straight feel his spur.
This new judge awakes me all the penalties
Which have, like unscour'd armour, hung by the wall
So long that fourteen zodiacs have gone round
And none of them been worn; and, for a name,
Now puts the drowsy and neglected act
Freshly on me: 'tis surely for a name.

Lucio
I warrant it is. Send after the duke and appeal
to him.

Claudio
I have done so, but he's not to be found.
I prithee, Lucio, do me this kind service:
This day my sister should the cloister enter

Acquaint her with the danger of my state:
Implore her, in my voice, that she make friends
To the strict deputy; for in her youth
There is a prone and speechless dialect,
Such as moves men; and well she can persuade.

Lucio
I'll to her.

Claudio
                I thank you, good friend Lucio.

Lucio
Within two hours.

Exit **Lucio**.

Enter **Angelo**, **Escalus** *and* **Justice**.

Angelo
                Where is the prisoner?

Provost
He is here, if it like your honour.

Escalus
Let us be keen, and rather cut a little,
Than fall, and bruise to death. Alas, this gentleman
Whom I would save, had a most noble father!
Have we not all, at sometime in our lives
Err'd in this point which now you censure him,
And pulled the law upon us.

Angelo
'tis one thing to be tempted, Escalus,
Another thing to fall: what knows the laws
That thieves do pass on thieves?
When I, that censure him, do so offend,
Let mine own judgment pattern out my death,
And nothing come in partial. Sir, he must die.

Escalus
Be it as your wisdom will.

Angelo

Claudio, you are to be executed:
Let it be by nine to-morrow morning.
Bring him his confessor, let him be prepared.

Exit **Justice** *and* **Claudio**.

Provost

I crave your honour's pardon.
What shall be done, with the groaning Juliet?
She's very near her hour.

Angelo

Dispose of her
To some more fitter place, and that with speed.
Let her have needful, but not lavish, means.

Exit **Angelo**.

Escalus

What's a clock, think you?

Provost

Eleven, sir.

Escalus

I pray you, home to dinner with me.

Provost

I humbly thank you.

Escalus

It grieves me for the death of Claudio,
But there's no remedy.

Provost

Lord Angelo is severe.

Escalus

It is but needful.
But yet, poor Claudio. Come sir.

Exeunt.

Scene Four: The Retreat

Isabel *and* **Francisca**.

Isabel

And have you nuns no farther privileges?

Francisca

Are not these large enough?

Isabel

Yes, truly; I speak not as desiring more;
But rather wishing a more strict restraint.

Lucio (*without*)

Ho! Peace be in this place!

Isabel

Who's that which calls?

Francisca

Turn you the key, and know his business of him;
You may, I may not; you are yet unsworn.
If I speak I must not show my face,
Or if I show my face, I must not speak.

Exit **Francisca**.

Isabel

Peace and prosperity! Who is't that calls?

Enter **Lucio**.

Lucio

Can you bring me to the sight of Isabel,
Sister to the unhappy Claudio.

Isabel

I am that Isabel and his sister.

Lucio

Gentle and fair, your brother kindly greets you:
Not to be weary with you, he's in prison.

Isabel

For what?

Lucio

For that which, if myself might be his judge,
He should receive his punishment in thanks:
He hath got his friend with child.

Isabel

Sir, make me not your story.

Lucio

                    It is true.
I hold you as a thing ensky'd and sainted.
By your renouncement an immortal spirit,
And to be talk'd with in sincerity.

Isabel

You do blaspheme the good in mocking me.

Lucio

Do not believe it. Fewness and truth, 'tis thus:
Your brother and his lover have embraced.

Isabel

Some one with child by him? My cousin Juliet?

Lucio

Your cousin?

Isabel

               Adoptedly.

Lucio

                    She it is.

Isabel

O, let him marry her.

Lucio

               This is the point.
The duke is very strangely gone from hence;
And with full line of his authority,

Governs Lord Angelo; a man whose blood
Is very snow-broth; one who never feels.
Giving fear to liberty, he picked out an act,
Under whose heavy sense your brother's life
Falls into forfeit: he arrests him on it;
And follows close the letter of the law,
To make him an example. All hope is gone,
Unless you have the grace by your fair prayer
To soften Angelo.

Isabel

Doth he so seek his life?

Lucio

                    The provost hath
A warrant for his execution.

Isabel

Alas! what poor ability's in me
To do him good?

Lucio

                Try the power you have.

Isabel

My power? Alas, I doubt –

Lucio

                  Our doubts are traitors
And make us lose the good we oft might win
By fearing to attempt. When young ones kneel
Men give like gods.

Isabel

                I'll see what I can do.

Lucio

But speedily.

Isabel

            I will about it straight;

No longer staying but to give Francisca
Notice of my affair. I humbly thank you.

Lucio

I take my leave of you.

Isabel

Good sir, adieu.

Exeunt.

Act Two

Scene One: The Courtroom

Angelo *and* **Provost**.

Angelo
Now, what's the matter. Provost?

Provost
Is it your will Claudio shall die tomorrow?

Angelo
Did not I tell thee yea? Hadst thou not order?
Why dost thou ask again?

Provost
                      Lest I might be too rash:
Under your good correction, I have seen,
When, after execution, judgment hath
Repented o'er his doom.

Angelo
Do you your office, or give up your place.

Provost
Here is the sister of the man condemn'd
Desires access to you.

Angelo
                Hath he a sister?

Provost
Ay, my good lord.

Angelo
               Well, let her be admitted.

Exit **Provost**.

Re-enter **Provost** *with* **Isabel** *and* **Lucio**.

Provost
God save your honour!

Angelo (*to* **Provost**)

> Stay a little while.
> (*To* **Isabel**.) You're welcome: what's your will?

Isabel

> I am a woeful suitor to your honour,
> Please but your honour hear me.

Angelo

> Well, what's your suit?

Isabel

> There is a vice that most I do abhor,
> And most desire should meet the blow of justice;
> For which I would not plead, but that I must;
> For which I must not plead, but that I am
> At war 'twixt will and will not.

Angelo

> Well, the matter?

Isabel

> I have a brother is condemn'd to die:
> I do beseech you, let it be his fault,
> And not my brother.

Provost (*aside*)

> Heaven give thee moving graces!

Isabel

> Must he needs die?

Angelo

> Maiden, there's no remedy.

Isabel

> I had a brother, then. Heaven keep your honour!

Lucio (*aside to* **Isabel**)

> Give't not o'er so: to him again, entreat him;
> Kneel down before him. You are too cold.

Isabel

Yet I do think that you might pardon him,
And neither heaven nor man grieve at the mercy.

Angelo

I will not do't.

Isabel

But can you, if you would?

Angelo

Look, what I will not, that I cannot do.

Isabel

But might you do't, and do the world no wrong,
If so your heart were touch'd with that remorse
As mine is to him?

Angelo

He's sentenced; 'tis too late.

Lucio (*aside to* **Isabel**)

You are too cold.

Isabel

Too late? why, no; I, that do speak a word.
May call it back again. Well, believe this,
No ceremony that to great ones 'longs,
Not the king's crown, nor the deputed sword,
The marshal's truncheon, nor the judge's robe,
Become them with one half so good a grace
As mercy does.

Angelo

Pray you, be gone.

Isabel

I would to heaven I had your potency,
And you were Isabel! Should it then be thus?
No: I would tell what 'twere to be a judge,
And what a prisoner.

Lucio (*aside to* **Isabel**)
Ay, touch him; there's the vein.

Angelo
Your brother is a forfeit of the law,
And you but waste your words.

Isabel
                    Alas, alas!
Why, all the souls that were, were forfeit once.
And He that might the vantage best have took
Found out the remedy. How would you be,
If He, which is the top of judgment, should
But judge you as you are? O, think on that;
And mercy then will breathe within your lips
Like man new made.

Angelo
                    Be you content with this:
It is the law, not I condemn your brother:
Were he my kinsman, brother, or my son,
It should be thus with him: he must die tomorrow.

Isabel
To-morrow! O, that's sudden! Spare him, spare him!
He's not prepared for death. Even for our kitchens
We kill the fowl of season: bethink you;
Who is it that hath died for this offence?
There's many have committed it.

Lucio (*aside to* **Isabel**)
Ay, well said.

Angelo
The law hath not been dead, though it hath slept:
Now 'tis awake, takes note of what is done,
And like a prophet, looks in a glass
That shows what future evils to be hatched and born
Are now to have no successive degrees,
But here they live to end.

Isabel

                        Yet show some pity.

Angelo

    I show it most of all when I show justice;
    For then I pity those I do not know.
    Your brother dies to-morrow; be content.

Isabel

    So you must be the first that gives this sentence,
    And he, that suffers. O, it is excellent
    To have a giant's strength; but it is tyrannous
    To use it like a giant.

Lucio (*aside to* **Isabel**)

    That's well said.

Isabel

    Could great ones thunder
    As Jove himself does, Jove would ne'er be quiet,
    For every pelting, petty officer
    Would use his heaven for thunder;
    Nothing but thunder! But man, proud man,
    Dressed in a little brief authority,
    Most ignorant of what he's most assured,
    His glassy essence, like an angry ape,
    Plays such fantastic tricks before high heaven
    As make the angels weep.

Lucio (*aside to* **Isabel**)

    O, to him, to him, wench! He will relent; he's coming;
    I perceive 't.

Isabel

    We cannot weigh our brother with ourself:
    Great men may jest with saints; 'tis wit in them,
    But in the less foul profanation.

Lucio

    More of that, maid.

Isabel

Go to your bosom;
Knock there, and ask your heart what it doth know
That's like my brother's fault: if it confess
A natural guiltiness such as is his,
Let it not sound a thought upon your tongue
Against my brother's life.

Angelo (*aside*)

She speaks, and 'tis
Such sense, that my sense breeds with it.
(*To* **Isabel**.) Fare you well.

Isabel

Gentle judge, turn back.

Angelo

Come again tomorrow.

Isabel

Hark how I'll bribe you: your honour, turn back.

Angelo

How! Bribe me?

Isabel

Ay, with such gifts that heaven shall share with you.

Lucio (*aside to* **Isabel**)

You had marr'd all else.

Isabel

Not with tested gold; but with true prayers
That shall fly up to heaven and enter there
Ere sun-rise. Prayers from a fasting soul.

Angelo

Well; come to me to-morrow.

Lucio (*aside to* **Isabel**)

Go to; 'tis well: away!

Isabel

Heaven keep your honour safe!

Angelo

Amen.
(*Aside.*) For I am that way going to temptation,
Where prayers cross.

Isabel

At what hour to-morrow
Shall I attend your honour?

Angelo

At any time 'fore noon.

Isabel

'Save your honour!

Exeunt **Isabel**, **Lucio** *and* **Provost**.

Angelo

From thee, even from thy virtue!
What's this, what's this? Is this her fault or mine?
The tempter or the tempted, who sins most?
Ha! Can it be? Having waste ground enough,
Shall we desire to raze the sanctuary
And pitch our evils there? O, fie, fie, fie!
What dost thou, or what art thou, Angelo?
Dost thou desire her foully for those things
That make her good? O, let her brother live!
Thieves for their robbery have authority
When judges steal themselves. What, do I love her,
That I desire to hear her speak again,
And feast upon her eyes? What is't I dream on?
O cunning enemy, that, to catch a saint,
With saints dost bait thy hook! Most dangerous
Is that temptation that doth goad us on
To sin in loving virtue. Even till now,
When men were fond, I smiled and wonder'd how.

Exit **Angelo**.

Scene Two: The Prison

Duke, *disguised as a friar, and* **Provost**.

Duke

Hail to you, Provost! So I think you are.

Provost

I am the provost. What's your will, good friar?

Duke

Bound by my charity and my blest order,
I come to visit the afflicted spirits
Here in the prison. Do me the common right
To let me see them.

Provost

I would do more than that, if more were needful.

Enter **Claudio**.

Duke

When must he die?

Provost

As I do think, tomorrow.

Duke

Is there a hope of pardon?

Claudio

The miserable have no other medicine
But only hope:
I've hope to live, and am prepared to die.

Duke

Be absolute for death; either death or life
Shall thereby be the sweeter. Reason thus with life:
If I do lose thee, I do lose a thing
That none but fools would keep: a breath thou art,
Servile to all the skyey influences,
That dost this habitation, where thou keep'st,
Hourly afflict: merely, thou art death's fool;

For him thou labour'st by thy flight to shun
And yet runn'st toward him still. Thy best of rest is sleep,
And that thou oft provokest; yet grossly fear'st
Thy death, which is no more. Thou art not thyself;
For thou exist'st on many a thousand grains
That issue out of dust. Happy thou art not;
For what thou hast not, still thou strivest to get,
And what thou hast, forget'st. Thou hast nor youth nor
age,
But, as it were, an after-dinner's sleep,
Dreaming on both; for all thy blessed youth
Becomes as aged, and doth beg the alms
Of palsied eld; and when thou art old and rich,
Thou hast neither heat, affection, limb, nor beauty,
To make thy riches pleasant. What's yet in this
That bears the name of life? Yet in this life
Lie hid more thousand deaths: yet death we fear,
That makes these odds all even.

Claudio

                         I humbly thank you.
To sue to live, I find I seek to die;
And, seeking death, find life: let it come on.

Exeunt.

Scene Three: The Courtroom

Enter **Angelo**.

Angelo

When I would pray and think, I think and pray
To several subjects. Heaven hath my empty words;
Whilst my invention, hearing not my tongue,
Anchors on Isabel: Heaven in my mouth,
As if I did but only chew his name;
And in my heart the strong and swelling evil
Of my conception. O place, O form,
How often dost thou with thy case, thy habit,

Wrench awe from fools and tie the wiser souls
To thy false seeming! Blood, thou art blood.

Enter **Provost**.

How now! who's there?

Provost
One Isabel desires access to you.

Angelo
Teach her the way.

Exit **Provost**.
                              O heavens!
Why does my blood thus muster to my heart,
Making both it unable for itself,
And dispossessing all my other parts
Of necessary fitness?
So play the foolish throngs with one that swoons;
Come all to help him, and so stop the air
By which he should revive.

Enter **Isabel**.

                              How now, fair maid?

Isabel
I am come to know your pleasure.

Angelo
That you might know it, would much better please me
Than to demand what 'tis. Your brother cannot live.

Isabel
Even so. Heaven keep your honour!

Angelo
Yet may he live awhile; and, it may be,
As long as you or I yet he must die.

Isabel
Under your sentence?

Angelo
                              Yea.

Isabel

When, I beseech you?

Angelo

Ha! fie, these filthy vices! It were as good
To pardon him that hath from nature stolen
A man already made, as to remit
His saucy sweetness, that do coin heaven's image
In stamps that are forbid.

Isabel

'Tis set down so in heaven, but not in earth.

Angelo

Say you so? then I shall pose you quickly.
Which had you rather, that the most just law
Now took your brother's life; or, to redeem him,
Give up your body to such sweet uncleanness
As Juliet that he hath stain'd?

Isabel

Sir, believe this,
I had rather give my body than my soul.

Angelo

I talk not of your soul.

Isabel

How say you?

Angelo

I, now the voice of the recorded law,
Pronounce a sentence on your brother's life:
Might there not be a charity in sin
To save this brother's life?

Isabel

Please you to do't,
I'll take it as a peril to my soul,
It is no sin at all, but charity.

Angelo

Pleased you to do't at peril of your soul,
Were equal poise of sin and charity.

Isabel

That I do beg his life, if it be sin,
Heaven let me bear it! Your granting of my suit,
If that be sin, I'll make it my morn prayer
To have it added to the faults of mine,
And nothing of your answer.

Angelo

                              Nay, but hear me.
Your sense pursues not mine: either you are ignorant,
Or seem so craftily; and that's not good.
To be received plain, I'll speak more gross:
Your brother is to die.

Isabel

So.

Angelo

And his offence is so, as it appears,
Accountant to the law upon that pain.

Isabel

True.

Angelo

What should happen if that you, his sister,
Finding yourself desired of such a person,
Whose credit with the judge, or own great place,
Could fetch your brother from the manacles
Of the all-binding law; and that there were
No earthly mean to save him, but that either
You must lay down the treasures of your body
To this supposed, or else to let him suffer;
What would you do?

Isabel

As much for my poor brother as myself:
That is, were I under the terms of death,

The impression of keen whips I'd wear as rubies,
And strip myself to death, as to a bed
That longing have been sick for, ere I'd yield
My body up to shame.

Angelo

Then must your brother die.

Isabel

And 'twere the cheaper way:
Better it were a brother died at once,
Than that a sister, by redeeming him,
Should die for ever.

Angelo

Were not you then as cruel as the sentence
That you have slander'd so?

Isabel

Ignomy in ransom and free pardon
Are of two houses: lawful mercy
Is nothing kin to foul redemption.

Angelo

You seem'd of late to make the law a tyrant;
And rather proved the sliding of your brother
A merriment than a vice.

Isabel

O, pardon me, my lord; it oft falls out,
To have what we would have, we speak not what we mean:
I something do excuse the thing I hate,
For his advantage that I dearly love.

Angelo

We are all frail.

Isabel

Men are frail too.

Angelo

I think it well:
Since I suppose we are made to be no stronger

Than faults may shake our frames, let me be bold;
I do arrest your words. Be that you are,
That is, a woman; if you be more, you're none;
If you be one, as you are well express'd
By all external warrants, show it now,
By putting on the destined livery.

Isabel

I have no tongue but one: gentle my lord,
Let me entreat you speak the former language.

Angelo

Plainly conceive, I love you.

Isabel

My brother did love Juliet,
And you tell me that he shall die for it.

Angelo

He shall not, Isabel, if you give me love.

Isabel

I know your virtue hath a licence in't,
Which seems a little fouler than it is,
To pluck on others.

Angelo

                    Believe me, on mine honour,
My words express my purpose.

Isabel

Ha! little honour to be much believed,
And most pernicious purpose! Seeming, seeming!
I will proclaim thee, Angelo; look for't:
Sign me a present pardon for my brother,
Or with an outstretch'd throat I'll tell the world aloud
What thou art.

Angelo

                    Who will believe thee, Isabel?
My unsoil'd name, the austereness of my life,
My vouch against you, and my place i' the state,

Will so your accusation overweigh,
That you shall stifle in your own report
And smell of calumny. I have begun,
And now I give my sensual race the rein:
Fit thy consent to my sharp appetite;
By yielding up thy body to my will;
Or else your brother must not only die,
But thy unkindness shall his death draw out
To lingering sufferance. Answer me to-morrow,
Or, by the affection that now guides me most,
I'll prove a tyrant to him. As for you,
Say what you can, my false o'erweighs your true.

Exit **Angelo**.

Isabel

To whom should I complain? Did I tell this,
Who would believe me? I'll to my brother:
Though he hath fallen by prompture of the blood,
Yet hath he in him such a mind of honour
That, had he twenty heads to tender down
On twenty bloody blocks, he'd yield them up,
Before his sister should her body stoop
To such abhorr'd pollution.
Then, Isabel, live chaste, and, brother, die:
More than our brother is our chastity.
I'll tell him yet of Angelo's request,
And fit his mind to death, for his soul's rest.

Exit **Isabel**.

Act Three

Scene One: The Prison

Enter **Isabel** *to greet the* **Provost** *as the* **Duke***, disguised as before, leaves* **Claudio***.*

Isabel
Peace here; grace and good company!

Provost
Who's there?

Duke
Dear sir, ere long I'll visit you again.

Isabel
My business is a word or two with Claudio.

Claudio
Most holy sir, I thank you.

Provost
And very welcome. Look, signior, here's
your sister.

Duke
Provost, a word with you.

Provost
As many as you please.

Duke
Let me to hear them speak, where I may be concealed.

Exeunt **Duke** *and* **Provost***.*

Claudio
Now, sister, what's the comfort?

Isabel
Why, as all comforts are; most good, most good indeed.
Lord Angelo, having affairs to heaven,
Intends you for his swift ambassador,
Therefore your best appointment make with speed;
To-morrow you set on.

Claudio

Is there no remedy?

Isabel

None, but such remedy as, to save a head,
To cleave a heart in twain.

Claudio

But is there any?

Isabel

Yes, brother, you may live:
There is a devilish mercy in the judge,
If you'll implore it, that will free your life,
But fetter you till death.

Claudio

But in what nature?

Isabel

In such a one as, you consenting to't,
Would bark your honour from that trunk you bear,
And leave you naked.

Claudio

Let me know the point.

Isabel

O, I do fear thee, Claudio; Darest thou die?
The sense of death is most in apprehension;
And the poor beetle, that we tread upon,
In corporal sufferance finds a pang as great
As when a giant dies.

Claudio

Why give you me this shame?
Think you I can a resolution fetch
From flowery tenderness? If I must die,
I will encounter darkness as a bride,
And hug it in mine arms.

Isabel

There spake my brother; there my father's grave
Did utter forth a voice. Yes, thou must die:
Thou art too noble to conserve a life
In base cowardice. This outward-sainted deputy,
Whose settled visage and deliberate word
Nips youth i' the head, is yet a devil.
His filth within being cast, he would appear
A pond as deep as hell.

Claudio

The pious Angelo!

Isabel

If I would yield him my virginity,
Thou mightst be freed.

Claudio

O heavens! it cannot be.

Isabel

O, were it but my life,
I'd throw it down for your deliverance
As frankly as a pin.

Claudio

Thanks, dear Isabel.

Isabel

Be ready, Claudio, for your death tomorrow.

Claudio

Yes. Has he affections in him?
Sure, it is no sin,
Or of the deadly seven, it is the least.

Isabel

Which is the least?

Claudio

O Isabel!

Isabel

What says my brother?

Claudio

Death is a fearful thing.

Isabel

And shamed life a hateful.

Claudio

Ay, but to die, and go we know not where;
To lie in cold obstruction and to rot;
This sensible warm motion to become
A kneaded clod; and the delighted spirit
To bathe in fiery floods, or to reside
In thrilling region of thick-ribbed ice;
To be imprison'd in the viewless winds,
And blown with restless violence round about
The pendent world; or to be worse than worst
Of those that lawless and incertain thought
Imagine howling: 'tis too horrible!
The weariest and most loathed worldly life
That age, ache, penury and imprisonment
Can lay on nature is a paradise
To what we fear of death.

Isabel

Alas, alas!

Claudio

Sweet sister, let me live:
What sin you do to save Claudio's life,
Nature dispenses with the deed so far
That it becomes a virtue.

Isabel

O faithless coward!
Wilt thou be made a man out of my vice?
Is't not a kind of incest, to take life
From thine own sister's shame? What should I think?
Die, perish! Might but my bending down

Reprieve thee from thy fate, it should proceed:
I'll pray a thousand prayers for thy death,
No word to save thee.

Claudio

Nay, hear me, Isabel.

Isabel

O, fie, fie, fie!
Thy sin's not accidental, but a trade.
Mercy to thee would prove itself a bawd:
'Tis best thou diest quickly.

Claudio

O hear me, Isabel!

Re-enter **Duke**.

Duke

Vouchsafe a word, young sister, but one word.

Isabel

What is your will?

Duke

Might you dispense with your leisure, I would by and by
have some speech with you: the satisfaction I would
require is likewise your own benefit.

Isabel

I have no superfluous leisure; my stay must be stolen out
of other affairs; but I will attend you awhile.

Exit **Isabel**.

Duke

Son, I have overheard what hath passed between you and
your sister. Angelo had never the purpose to corrupt her;
only he hath made a trial of her virtue. I am confessor to
Angelo, and I know this to be true; therefore prepare
yourself to death: go to your knees and make ready.

Claudio

Let me ask my sister pardon. I am so out of love with life
that I will pray to be rid of it.

Duke

Hold you there: farewell.

Exit **Claudio**.

Provost, a word with you!

Re-enter **Provost**.

Provost

What's your will, father?

Duke

That now you are come, you will be gone. Leave me
awhile with the maid: no loss shall touch her by my
company.

Provost

In good time.

Exit **Provost**. *Enter* **Isabel**.

Duke

The assault that Angelo hath made to you, fortune hath
conveyed to my understanding. He made trial of you only.
Therefore fasten your ear on my advisings: to the love I
have in doing good, a remedy presents itself. I do make
myself believe that you may most do a poor wronged lady
a merited benefit; redeem your brother from the angry
law; do no stain to your own gracious person; and much
please the absent duke, if peradventure he shall ever
return to have hearing of this business.

Isabel

Let me hear you speak farther. I have spirit to do
anything that appears not foul in the truth of my spirit.

Duke

Virtue is bold, and goodness never fearful. Have you not
heard speak of Mariana, whose brother Frederick, some
five years since, miscarried at sea?

Isabel

I have heard of the lady, and good words went with her name.

Duke

She should this Angelo have married; was bound to him by oath, and the nuptial appointed. Between which time, her brother Frederick lost his ship and with it all his fortune and the dowry of his sister.

Isabel

Can this be so? Did Angelo so leave her?

Duke

Left her in tears, and dried not one of them with his comfort; swallowed his vows whole, pretending in her discoveries of dishonour: and he, a marble to her tears, is washed with them, but relents not.

Isabel

What corruption in this life, that it will let this man live!

Duke

The cure of this not only saves your brother, but keeps you from dishonour.

Isabel

Show me how, good father.

Duke

This Mariana hath yet in her the continuance of her first affection: his unjust unkindness, that in all reason should have quenched her love, hath, like an impediment in the current, made it more violent and unruly. Go you to Angelo: answer his requiring with a plausible obedience. Agree with his demands to the point; only that your stay with him may not be long; that the time may have all shadow and silence in it; and the place answer to convenience. This being granted (and now follows all) we shall advise this wronged maid to go in your place. Here,

by this, is your brother saved, your honour untainted, the
poor Mariana advantaged, and the corrupt Angelo scaled.
What think you of it?

Isabel

The image of it gives me content already; and I trust it
will grow to a most prosperous perfection.

Duke

It lies much in your holding up. Haste you speedily to
Angelo: if for this night he entreat you to his bed, give
him promise of satisfaction. I will presently to Saint
Luke's. There, at the moated grange, resides this dejected
Mariana. At that place call upon me; and dispatch with
Angelo, that it may be quickly.

Isabel

I thank you for this comfort. Fare you well,
good father.

Exeunt.

Scene Two: The Courtroom

Duke, *disguised as before, the* **Justice** *with* **Pompey**.

Justice

Come your way, madam. 'Bless you, good friar.

Duke

And you. What offence hath this woman made you, sir?

Justice

Marry sir she hath offended the law that she will needs
buy and sell men and women like beasts.

Duke

Canst thou believe thy living is a life, so stinkingly
depending? Go mend, go mend.

Pompey

Indeed, it does stink in some sort, sir; but yet, sir, I would
prove –

Duke

Take her to prison, officer.

Justice

She must before the deputy, sir; he has given her
warning: the deputy cannot abide a whoremaster.

Enter **Lucio**.

Pompey

I spy comfort; I cry bail. Here's a friend of mine.

Lucio

How now, noble Pompey! What, at the wheels of Caesar?
What reply, ha? Is the world as it was, man? Which is the
way? Is it sad, and few words? Or how? The trick of it? Art
going to prison, Pompey?

Pompey

Yes, faith, sir.

Lucio

For debt Pompey or how?

Pompey

For being a bawd, for being a bawd.

Lucio

Why, 'tis not amiss, Pompey. Farewell.

Pompey

I hope, sir, your good worship will be my bail.

Lucio

No, indeed, will I not, Pompey. Adieu, trusty Pompey.
'Bless you, friar.

Duke

And you.

Justice

Come your ways, madam; come.

Pompey

You will not bail me, then, sir?

Lucio

Go to kennel, Pompey; go.

Exeunt **Pompey** *and* **Justice**.

What news, friar, of the duke?

Duke

I know none. Can you tell me of any?

Lucio

It was a mad fantastical trick of him to steal from the state, and usurp the beggary he was never born to. Lord Angelo dukes it well in his absence.

Duke

He does well in 't.

Lucio

A little more lenity to lechery would do no harm in him, friar.

Duke

It is too general a vice, and severity must cure it.

Lucio

They say this Angelo was not made by man and woman: is it true, think you?

Duke

How should he be made, then?

Lucio

Some report a sea-maid spawned him; some, that he was begot between two stock-fishes. But it is certain that when he makes water his urine is congealed ice; that I know to be true.

Duke

You are pleasant, sir.

Lucio

Why, what a ruthless thing is this in him, for the rebellion
of a codpiece to take away the life of a man! Would the
duke that is absent have done this? Ere he would have
hanged a man for the getting a hundred bastards, he
would have paid for the nursing a thousand: he had some
feeling of the sport: he knew the service, and that
instructed him to mercy.

Duke

I never heard the absent duke much detected for women;
he was not inclined that way.

Lucio

O, sir, you are deceived.

Duke

'Tis not possible.

Lucio

Who, not the duke? Yes, a fifty year old beggar; and his
use was to put a ducat in her clack-dish. He would be
drunk too; that let me inform you.

Duke

Either this is the envy in you, folly, or mistaking. Let him
be but testimonied, and he shall appear to the envious a
scholar, a statesman and a soldier.

Lucio

Sir, I know him, and I love him.

Duke

Love talks with better knowledge, and knowledge with
dearer love.

Lucio

Come, sir, I know what I know.

Duke

I can hardly believe that, since you know not what you speak. I pray you, your name?

Lucio

Sir, my name is Lucio; well known to the duke.

Duke

He shall know you better, sir, if I may live to report you.

Lucio

I fear you not. But no more of this. Canst thou tell if Claudio die to-morrow or no?

Duke

Why should he die, sir?

Lucio

Why? For filling a bottle with a tundish. I would the duke we talk of were returned again: the ungenitured deputy will unpeople the province with his continency; sparrows must not build in his house-eaves, because they are lecherous. The duke yet would have dark deeds darkly answered; he would never bring them to light: would he were returned! Marry, this Claudio is condemned for untrussing. Farewell, good friar: I prithee, pray for me. The duke, I say to thee again, would mouth with a beggar, though she smelt brown bread and garlic: say that I said so. Farewell.

Exit **Lucio**.

Duke

Back-wounding calumny.

Enter **Escalus** *and* **Provost**, *with* **Mistress Overdone**.

Escalus

What? Before me again?

Mistress Overdone

Good my lord, be good to me; your honour is accounted a merciful man; good my lord.

Provost

A bawd of eleven years continuance, may it please your honour.

Mistress Overdone

My lord, this is one Lucio's information against me. Mistress Kate Keepdown was with child by him in the duke's time, he promised her marriage, his child is a year and a quarter old – I have kept it myself – and see how he goes about to abuse me.

Escalus

That fellow is a fellow of much licence, let him be called before us. Away with her to prison! Go to; no more words. Provost, Angelo will not be altered; Claudio must die to-morrow: let him be furnished with divines, and have all charitable preparation.

Provost

So please you, this friar hath been with him, and advised him for the entertainment of death.

Exeunt **Provost** *with* **Mistress Overdone**.

Escalus

Good even, good father.

Duke

Bliss and goodness on you!

Escalus

What news abroad i' the world?

Duke

None, but that there is so great a fever on goodness, that the dissolution of it must cure it. This news is old enough, yet it is every day's news. I pray you, sir, of what disposition was the duke?

Escalus

One that, above all other strifes, contended especially to know himself.

Duke

What pleasure was he given to?

Escalus

A gentleman of all temperance. But leave we him to his events, with a prayer they may prove prosperous; and let me desire to know how you find Claudio prepared. I am made to understand that you have lent him visitation.

Duke

He willingly humbles himself to the determination of justice, and is resolved to die.

Escalus

I have laboured for the poor gentleman to the extremest shore of my modesty: but my brother justice have I found so severe, that he hath forced me to tell him he is indeed Justice.

Duke

If his own life answer the straitness of his proceeding, it shall become him well; wherein if he chance to fail, he hath sentenced himself.

Escalus

I am going to visit the prisoner. Fare you well.

Duke

Peace be with you!

Exeunt.

Act Four

Scene One: The Retreat

Enter **Mariana** *and* **Thomas**.

A song:

> Take oh, take those lips away,
> That so sweetly were forsworn;
> And those eyes, the break of day,
> Lights that do mislead the morn:
> But my kisses bring again, bring again;
> Seals of love, but sealed in vain, sealed in vain.

Enter **Duke**, *disguised as before.*

Thomas

Let me excuse me.

Duke

I cry you mercy, sir.

Exit **Thomas**.

I pray, you, tell me, hath any body inquired for me here to-day? Much upon this time have I promised here to meet.

Mariana

You have not been inquired after: I have sat here all day.

Enter **Isabel**.

Duke

I do constantly believe you. The time is come even now. I shall crave your forbearance a little: may be I will call upon you anon, for some advantage to yourself.

Mariana

I am always bound to you.

Exit **Mariana**.

Duke

Very well met, and well come.
What is the news from this good deputy?

Isabel

He hath a garden walled in with brick,
That makes his opening with this little key:
There have I made my promise
Upon the heavy middle of the night.
I have possess'd him my most stay
Can be but brief; for I have made him know
I have a servant comes with me along,
That stays upon me, whose persuasion is
I come about my brother.

Duke

                         'Tis well borne up.
I have not yet made known to Mariana
A word of this. What, ho! within! come forth!

Re-enter **Mariana**.

I pray you, be acquainted with this maid;
She comes to do you good.

Mariana

I do desire the like.

Duke

Do you persuade yourself that I respect you?

Mariana

Good friar, I know you do, and have found it.

Duke

Take, then, this your companion by the hand,
Who hath a story ready for your ear.
I shall attend your leisure: but make haste;
The vaporous night approaches.

Mariana

Will't please you walk aside?

Exeunt **Mariana** *and* **Isabel**.

Duke

O place and greatness! millions of false eyes
Are stuck upon thee: volumes of report
Run with these false and most contrarious quests
Upon thy doings: thousand escapes of wit
Make thee the father of their idle dreams
And rack thee in their fancies.

Re-enter **Mariana** *and* **Isabel**.

Welcome, how agreed?

Isabel

She'll take the enterprise upon her, father,
If you advise it.

Duke

It is not only my consent,
But my entreaty too.

Isabel

Little have you to say
When you depart from him, but, soft and low,
'Remember now my brother.'

Mariana

Fear me not.

Duke

Nor, gentle daughter, fear you not at all.
He is your husband on a pre-contract.
To bring you thus together, 'tis no sin.

Exeunt.

Scene Two: The Prison

Enter **Provost** *and* **Duke**, *disguised as before.*

Duke

Good Provost! Who called here of late?

Provost

None, since the curfew rung.

Duke

Not Isabel?

Provost

No.

Duke

She will, then, before long.

Provost

What comfort is for Claudio?

Duke

There's some in hope.

Provost

It is a bitter deputy.

Duke

Not so, not so; his life is parallel'd
Even with the stroke and line of his great justice.
This is Angelo's man.

Exit **Provost**.

And here comes Claudio's pardon.

Re-enter **Provost**.

Now, sir, what news?
Pray you, let's hear.

Provost (*reads*)

'Whatsoever you may hear to the contrary, let Claudio be
executed by four of the clock. Let this be duly performed;
with a thought that more depends on it than we must yet
deliver. Thus fail not to do your office, as you will answer
it at your peril.' What say you to this, sir?

Duke

I will lay myself in hazard. Claudio, whom here you have
warrant to execute, is no greater forfeit to the law than

Angelo who hath sentenced him. To prove this, I crave
but four days' respite; for the which you are to do me
both a present and a dangerous courtesy.

Provost

Pray, sir, in what?

Duke

In the delaying death.

Provost

Alack, how may I do it, having the hour limited, and an
express command, under penalty. Pardon me, good
father; it is against my oath.

Duke

Were you sworn to the duke, or to the deputy?

Provost

To him, and to his substitutes.

Duke

Since I see you fearful, I will go further than I meant.
Look you, sir, here is the hand and seal of the duke: you
know the character, I doubt not; and the signet is not
strange to you.

Provost

I know them both.

Duke

The contents of this is the return of the duke: you shall
find, within these two days he will be here. This is a thing
that Angelo knows not; for he this very day receives letters
of strange tenor; perchance of the duke's death. Look, the
unfolding star calls up the shepherd. Put not yourself into
amazement how these things should be: all difficulties are
but easy when they are known.

Provost

This shall be done, good father, presently.
And how shall we continue Claudio,
To save me from the danger that might come
If he were known alive?

Duke
Let this be done. Put him in a secret cell.

Provost
I am your free dependant.

Duke
Send news of his execution to Angelo.

Provost
I'll make all speed.

Exit **Provost**.

Isabel (*within*)
Peace, ho, be here!

Duke
The tongue of Isabel. She's come to know
If yet her brother's pardon be come hither:
But I will keep her ignorant of her good,
To comfort her despair when least expected.

Enter **Isabel**.

Duke
Good morning to you, fair and gracious daughter.

Isabel
The better, given me by so holy a man.
Hath yet the deputy sent my brother's pardon?

Duke
He hath released him, Isabel, from the world.

Isabel
Nay, but it is not so.

Duke
It is no other: show your wisdom, daughter,
In your close patience.

Isabel
O, I will to him and pluck out his eyes!

Duke

You shall not be admitted to his sight.

Isabel

Unhappy Claudio! wretched Isabel!
Injurious world! most damned Angelo!

Duke

This nor hurts him nor profits you a jot;
Forbear it therefore; give your cause to heaven.
The duke comes home tomorrow; nay, dry your eyes.
Escalus and Angelo, meet him at the court,
There to give up their power. You shall have revenge.
Tomorrow, then.

Isabel

                    Direct me, friar.

Duke

This provost here brings you before the duke.
And in the open court, shall you accuse him.
Command these fretting waters from your eyes
With a light heart. Who's here?

Enter **Lucio**.

Lucio

Good even. Friar, where's the provost?

Duke

Not within, sir.

Lucio

O dearest Isabel, I am pale at mine heart to see thine eyes
so red. But they say the duke will be here tomorrow. By
my troth, Isabel, I loved thy brother: if the old fantastical
duke of dark corners had been at home, he had lived.

Exit **Isabel**.

Duke

Sir, the duke is marvellous little beholding to your
reports.

Lucio

Friar, thou knowest not the duke so well as I do.

Duke

Well, you'll answer this one day. Fare ye well.

Lucio

Nay, tarry; I'll go along with thee. I can tell thee pretty tales of the duke.

Duke

You have told me too many of him already, sir.

Lucio

I was once before him for getting a wench with child.

Duke

Did you such a thing?

Lucio

Yes, marry, did I but I denied it; they would else have married me to the rotten whore.

Duke

Sir, your company is fairer than honest. Rest you well.

Lucio

By my troth, I'll go with thee to the lane's end. If bawdy talk offend you, we'll have very little of it. Nay, friar, I am a kind of burr; I shall stick.

Exeunt.

Act Five

Scene One: The Courtroom

Enter **Angelo**.

Angelo

> This deed unshapes me quite, makes me unpregnant
> And dull to all proceedings. A deflower'd maid!
> And by an eminent body that enforced
> The law against it! But that her tender shame
> Will not proclaim against her virgin loss,
> How might she tongue me! Yet reason dares her no;
> For my authority bears of a credent bulk,
> That no particular scandal once can touch
> But it confounds the breather. Would yet he had lived!
> Alack, when once our grace we have forgot,
> Nothing goes right: we would, and we would not.

Enter **Escalus**.

Escalus

> Every letter the duke hath writ contradicts the former.

Angelo

> In most uneven and distracted manner. His actions show
> much like to madness.

Escalus

> I guess not.

Angelo

> And why did he demand it proclaimed, an hour before
> his return, that if any crave redress of injustice, they
> should exhibit their petitions here?

Enter **Duke**.

Duke

> My very worthy judges, fairly met!
> Our old and faithful friend, we are glad to see you.

Angelo

Happy return be to your royal grace!

Duke

Many and hearty thankings to you both.
We have made inquiry of you; and we hear
Such goodness of your justice, that our soul
Cannot but yield you forth to public thanks.

Angelo

You make my bonds still greater.

Duke

Give me your hand,
And let the subject see, to make them know
That outward courtesies would fain proclaim
Favours that keep within.

Enter **Isabel** *with* **Justice** *and the* **Provost** *and* **Mariana** *with*
Thomas.

Provost

Now is your time: speak loud and kneel before him.

Isabel

Justice, O royal duke! Dishonour not your eye
By throwing it on any other object
Till you have heard me in my true complaint
And given me justice, justice, justice, justice!

Duke

Relate your wrongs; in what? By whom? Be brief.
Here is a worthy judge shall give you justice:
Reveal yourself to him.

Isabel

O worthy duke,
You bid me seek redemption of the devil:
Hear me yourself; for that which I must speak
Must either punish me, not being believed,
Or wring redress from you. Hear me, O hear me, here!

Angelo

My lord, her wits, I fear me, are not firm:
She hath been a suitor to me for her brother
Cut off by course of justice –

Isabel

By course of justice!

Angelo

And she will speak most bitterly and strange.

Isabel

Most strange, but yet most truly, will I speak:
That Angelo's forsworn; is it not strange?
That Angelo's a murderer; is 't not strange?
That Angelo is a violator;
Is it not strange and strange?

Duke

Nay, it is ten times strange.

Isabel

Nay, it is ten times true; for truth is truth
To the end of reckoning.

Duke

Away with her! Poor soul,
She speaks this in the infirmity of sense.

Isabel

O prince, I conjure thee, as thou believest
There is another comfort than this world,
That thou neglect me not, with that opinion
That I am touch'd with madness! 'Tis not impossible
That one may seem as shy, as grave, as just
As Angelo; even so may Angelo
Be an arch-villain.

Duke

Many that are not mad
Have, sure, more lack of reason. What would you say?

Isabel

> I am the sister of one Claudio,
> Condemn'd upon the act of fornication
> To lose his head; condemn'd by Angelo:
> I, was sent to by my brother; one Lucio
> As then the messenger –

Lucio

> That's I, an't like your grace:
> I came to her from Claudio, and desired her
> To try her gracious fortune with Lord Angelo
> For her poor brother's pardon.

Isabel

> That's he indeed.

Duke

> You were not bid to speak.

Lucio

> No, my good lord;
> Nor wish'd to hold my peace.

Duke

> I wish you now, then;
> Pray you, take note of it: and when you have
> A business for yourself, pray heaven you then
> Be perfect.

Lucio

> I warrant your honour.

Duke

> The warrant's for yourself; take heed to't.

Isabel

> This gentleman told somewhat of my tale –

Lucio

> Right.

Duke

It may be right; but you are i' the wrong
To speak before your time. Proceed.

Isabel

I went
To this pernicious, villain deputy –

Duke

That's somewhat madly spoken.

Isabel

Pardon it; the phrase is to the matter.

Duke

Mended again. The matter; proceed.

Isabel

In brief, to set the needless process by,
How I persuaded, how I pray'd, and kneel'd,
How he repelled me, and how I replied –
For this was of much length – the vile conclusion
I now begin with grief and shame to utter:
He would not, but by gift of my chaste body
To his violent, intemperate lust,
Release my brother; and, after much debatement,
My sisterly remorse confutes mine honour,
And I did yield to him: but the next morn betimes,
His purpose done, he sends a warrant
For my poor brother's head.

Duke

This is most likely!

Isabel

O, that it were as like as it is true!

Duke

His integrity stands without blemish.
This imports no reason. Some one hath set you on:
Confess the truth, and say by whose advice
Thou camest here to complain.

Isabel

                                And is this all?
Then, O you blessed ministers above,
Keep me in patience, and with ripen'd time
Unfold the evil which is here wrapt up
In countenance! Heaven shield your grace from woe,
As I, thus wrong'd, hence unbelieved go!

Duke

I know you'd fain be gone. Shall we thus permit
A blasting and a scandalous breath to fall
On him so near us? This needs must be a practise.
Who knew of your intent and coming here?

Isabel

One that I would were here, a Friar.

Exit **Justice** *with* **Isabel**.

Duke

A ghostly father, belike. Who knows that Friar?

Lucio

My lord, I know him; I do not like the man
For certain words he spake against your grace.

Duke

Words against me? Let this friar be found.
Do you not smile at this, Lord Angelo?
O heaven, the vanity of wretched fools!
An officer! To prison with her.
In this I'll be impartial; be you judge
Of your own cause.

Mariana

My lord, let me speak.

Duke

                      Another witness?
First, let her show her face, and after speak.

Mariana
> Pardon, my lord; I will not show my face
> Until my husband bid me.

Duke
> What, are you married?

Mariana
> > No, my lord.

Duke
> A widow, then?

Mariana
> > Neither, my lord.

Duke
> Why, you are nothing then?

Mariana
> My lord; I do confess I ne'er was married;
> And yet I have known my husband; yet my husband
> Knows not that ever he knew me.

Lucio
> He was drunk then, my lord: it can be no better.

Duke
> For the benefit of silence, would thou wert so too!

Lucio
> Well, my lord.

Duke
> > You say your husband.

Mariana
> Why, just, my lord, and that is Angelo,
> Who thinks he knows that he ne'er knew my body,
> But knows he thinks that he knows Isabel's.

Angelo
> This is a strange abuse. Let's see thy face.

Mariana
My husband bids me; now I will unmask.
(*Unveiling*.) This is that face, thou cruel Angelo,
Which once thou sworest was worth the looking on;
This is the hand which, with a vow'd contract,
Was fast belock'd in thine; this is the body
That took away the match from Isabel,
And did supply thee at thy garden-house
In her imagined person.

Duke
                                 Know you this woman?

Lucio
Carnally, he says.

Duke
                 Sirrah, no more!

Lucio
Enough, my lord.

Angelo
My lord, I must confess I know this woman:
And five years since there was some speech of marriage
Betwixt myself and her; which was broke off,
Partly for that her promised proportions
Came short of composition, but in chief
For that her reputation was disvalued
In levity: since which time of five years
I never spake with her, saw her, nor heard from her,
Upon my faith and honour.

Mariana
                         Noble prince,
As there comes light from heaven and words from breath,
As there is sense in truth and truth in virtue,
I am this man's wife as strongly
As words could make up vows: and, my good lord,
But Tuesday night last gone in's garden-house
He knew me as a wife.

Angelo

                  I did but smile till now:
Now, good my lord, give me the scope of justice
My patience here is touch'd. I do perceive
These poor informal creatures are no more
But instruments of some more mightier member
That sets them on: let me have way, my lord,
To find this practise out.

Duke

                  Ay, with my heart.
You, Lord Escalus; lend him your kind pains
To find out this abuse, whence 'tis derived.
There is another friar that set them on;
Let him be sent for.

Thomas

Would he were here, my lord! For he indeed
Hath set these two here on to this complaint:
Your provost knows the place where he abides
And he may fetch him.

Duke

(*To the* **Provost**.) Go do it instantly.
And you, the noble and well-warranted Angelo,
Do with your injuries as seems you best,
In any chastisement: I for a while will leave you;
But stir not you till you have well determined
Upon these slanderers.

Escalus

My lord, we'll do it throughly.

Exit **Duke**.

Call that same Isabel here once again; I would speak
with her.
Pray you, my lord, give me leave to question; you
shall see how I'll handle her.

Lucio

Not better than he, by her own report.

Escalus

Say you?

Lucio

Marry, sir, I think, if you handled her privately,
she would sooner confess: perchance, publicly,
she'll be ashamed.

Escalus

I will go darkly to work with her.

Re-enter **Justice**, **Isabel**, **Provost** *and* **Duke**, *in his friar's habit.*

Come hither, Isabel: here's a gentlewoman denies all that
you have said.

Lucio

My lord, here comes the rascal.

Escalus

In very good time: speak not you to him till we call
upon you.

Lucio

Mum.

Escalus

Come, sir: did you set these two on to slander Lord
Angelo?

Duke

Where is the duke? 'tis he should hear me speak.

Escalus

The duke's in us; and we will hear you speak:
Look you speak justly.

Duke

                    Is the duke gone?
Then is your cause gone too. The duke's unjust.

Escalus

Why thou irreverent friar, slander to the state.

Lucio

This is the rascal; this is he I spoke of.

Angelo

What can you vouch against him, Signior Lucio?
Is this the man that you did tell us of?

Lucio

'Tis he, my lord. Come hither: do you know me?

Duke

I remember you, sir, by the sound of your voice: I met
you at the prison, in the absence of the duke.

Lucio

O, did you so? And do you remember what you said of the
duke?

Duke

Most notedly, sir.

Lucio

Do you so, sir? And was the duke a fleshmonger, a fool,
and a coward, as you then reported him to be?

Duke

You must, sir, change persons with me, ere you make that
my report: you, indeed, spoke so of him; and much more,
much worse.

Lucio

O thou damnable fellow!

Duke

I protest I love the duke as I love myself.

Angelo

Hark, how the villain would close now, after his
treasonable abuses!

Escalus

  Away with him to prison! Provost?

Lucio

  Come, sir; come, sir; come, sir; foh, sir!

Escalus

  Away with him to prison.

Lucio

  Why you, you lying rascal, you must be hooded, must
  you? Show your knave's visage, with a pox to you! Show
  your sheep-biting face, and be hanged an hour! Will't not
  off?

Pulls off the friar's hood, and discovers **Duke**.

  This may prove worse than hanging.

Duke (*to* **Escalus**)

  What you have spoke I pardon: sit you down:
  We'll borrow place of him.
  (*To* **Angelo**.) Now, by your leave.
  Hast thou or word, or wit, or impudence,
  That yet can do thee office? If thou hast,
  Rely upon it till my tale be heard,
  And hold no longer out.

Angelo

                O my dread lord,
  I should be guiltier than my guiltiness,
  To think I can be undiscernible,
  When I perceive your grace, like power divine,
  Hath look'd upon my passes. Then, good prince,
  No longer session hold upon my shame,
  But let my trial be mine own confession:
  Immediate sentence then and sequent death
  Is all the grace I beg.

Duke

Come hither, Mariana.
Say, wast thou e'er contracted to this woman?

Angelo

I was, my lord.

Duke

Go take her hence, and marry her instantly.
Do you the office, friar; which consummate,
Return him here again. Go with him, provost.

Exeunt **Angelo**, **Mariana**, **Thomas** *and* **Provost**.

Escalus

My lord, I am more amazed at his dishonour
Than at the strangeness of it.

Duke

Come hither, Isabel.
Your friar is now your prince: as I was then.

Isabel

O, give me pardon,
That I, your vassal, have employ'd and pain'd
Your unknown sovereignty!

Duke

You are pardon'd, Isabel:
And now, dear youth, be you as free to us.
Your brother's death, I know, sits at your heart;
And you may marvel why I obscured myself,
Labouring to save his life. But, peace be with him!
That life is better life, past fearing death,
Than that which lives to fear: make it your comfort,
So happy is your brother.

Isabel

I do, my lord.

Re-enter **Angelo**, **Mariana**, **Thomas** *and* **Provost**.

Duke

> For this new-married man approaching here,
> Whose salt imagination yet hath wrong'd
> Your well defended honour, you must pardon
> For Mariana's sake. But for your brother's life,
> The very mercy of the law cries out
> Most audible, even from his proper tongue,
> 'An Angelo for Claudio, death for death!'
> Haste still pays haste, and leisure answers leisure;
> Like doth quit like, and measure still for measure.
> Then, Angelo, thy fault's thus manifested;
> We do condemn thee to the very block
> Where Claudio stoop'd to death, and with like haste.
> Away with him!

Mariana

>   O my most gracious lord,
> I hope you will not mock me with a husband.

Duke

> I thought your marriage fit; for his possessions,
> Although by confiscation they are ours,
> We do instate and widow you withal,
> To buy you a better husband.

Mariana (*kneeling*)

>   O my dear lord,
> I crave no other, nor no better man.

Duke

> Never crave him; we are definitive.

Mariana

> O my good lord! Dear Isabel, take my part;
> Lend me your knees, and all my life to come
> I'll lend you all my life to do you service.

Duke

> Against all sense you do importune her.

Mariana

Isabel,
Dear Isabel, do yet but kneel by me;
Hold up your hands, say nothing; I'll speak all.
O Isabel will you not lend a knee?

Duke

He dies for Claudio's death.

Isabel (*kneeling*)

Most bounteous sir, I partly think
A due sincerity govern'd his deeds,
Till he did look on me: since it is so,
Let him not die

Duke

Stand up, I say.
I have bethought me of another fault.
Provost, how came it Claudio was beheaded
At an unusual hour?

Provost

It was commanded so.

Duke

Had you a special warrant for the deed?

Provost

No, my good lord; it was by private message.

Duke

For which I do discharge you of your office:
Give up your keys.

Provost

Pardon me, noble lord:
I thought it was a fault, but knew it not;
Yet did repent me, after more advice;
For testimony whereof, one in the prison,
That should by private order else have died,
I have reserved alive.

Duke

Go fetch him hither; let me look upon him.

Exit **Provost**.

Escalus

I am sorry, one so learned and so wise
Should slip so grossly, in the heat of blood.

Angelo

I am sorry that such sorrow I procure:
And so deep sticks it in my penitent heart
That I crave death more willingly than mercy.

Re-enter **Provost**, *with* **Claudio** *muffled*.

Provost

This is here a prisoner that I saved.
(*Unmuffles* **Claudio**.) As like almost to Claudio as himself.

Duke (*to* **Isabel**)

If he be like your brother, for his sake
Is he pardon'd; and, for your lovely sake,
Give me your hand and say you will be mine.
He is my brother too: but fitter time for that.
Well, Angelo, your evil quits you well:
I find an apt remission in myself;
And yet here's one in place I cannot pardon.
(*To* **Lucio**.) You, sirrah, that knew me for a fool, a coward,
One all of luxury, an ass, a madman;
Wherein have I so deserved of you?

Lucio

'Faith, my lord. If you will hang me for it, you may; but I
had rather it would please you I might be whipped.

Duke

Whipped first, sir, and hanged after.
Proclaim it, Justice, round about the city.
Is any woman wrong'd by this lewd fellow,
Whom he begot with child, let her appear,

And he shall marry her: the nuptial finish'd,
Let him be whipped and hang'd.

Lucio

Marrying a punk, my lord, is pressing to death, whipping,
and hanging.

Duke

Upon mine honour, thou shalt marry her.
Thy slanders I forgive, and therewithal
Remit thy other forfeits.

Exit **Justice** *with* **Lucio**.

She, Claudio, that you wrong'd, look you restore.
Joy to you, Mariana! Love her, Angelo.
Thanks, good friend Escalus, for thy much goodness:
There's more behind that is more gratulate.
Isabel, I have a motion much imports your good;
Whereto if you'll a willing ear incline,
What's mine is yours and what is yours is mine.

Exeunt all except **Isabel**, *who transforms from the novice to the deputy.*

Part Two

Act One

Scene One: The Courtroom

Enter **Duke**, **Escalus** *and* **Provost**.

Isabel
Always obedient to your grace's will,
I come to know your pleasure.

Duke
                    Isabel,
There is a kind of character in thy life,
That to the observer doth thy history
Fully unfold. But I do bend my speech
To one that can my part in her advertise;
Hold therefore, Isabel –
In our remove be thou at full ourself;
Mortality and mercy in Vienna
Live in thy tongue and heart: old Escalus,
Though first in question, is thy secondary.
Take thy commission.

Isabel
                    Now, good my lord,
Let there be some more test made of my metal,
Before so noble and so great a figure
Be stamp'd upon it.

Duke
                    No more evasion:
We have with a leavened and prepared choice
Proceeded to you; therefore take your honours.
Our haste from hence is of so quick condition
That it prefers itself and leaves unquestioned
Matters of needful value. We shall write to you,
How it goes with us. So, fare you well.

Isabel
May we bring you something on the way?

Duke

My haste admits it not. Give me your hand:
I'll privately away. I love the people,
But do not like to stage me to their eyes.
Once more, fare you well.

Escalus

Lead forth and bring you back in happiness!

Duke

I thank you. Fare you well.

Exit **Duke**.

Escalus

I shall desire you, ma'am, to give me leave
To have free speech with you: a power I have,
But of what strength I am not yet instructed.

Isabel

'Tis so with me. Let us withdraw together,
And we may soon our satisfaction have
Touching that point.

Escalus

                I'll wait upon your honour.

Exeunt.

Scene Two: The Retreat

Duke *and* **Thomas**.

Duke

My holy sir, I have deliver'd to Isabel,
My absolute power and place here in Vienna.
You will demand of me why I do this?

Thomas

Gladly, my lord.

Duke

> We have strict statutes and most biting laws,
> Which for this fourteen years we have let slip;
> We are more mock'd than fear'd; and our decrees,
> Dead to infliction, to themselves are dead;
> Thus liberty plucks justice by the nose;
> The baby beats the nurse, and quite athwart
> Goes all decorum.

Thomas

>   It rested in your grace
> To unloose this tied-up justice when you pleased:
> And it in you more dreadful would have seem'd
> Than in Isabel.

Duke

>   I do fear, too dreadful:
> Sith 'twas my fault to give the people scope,
> 'Twould be my tyranny to strike and gall them
> For what I bid them do. Therefore indeed, my father,
> I have on Isabel imposed the office.
> I will, as 'twere a member of your order,
> Behold her sway. Isabel is precise;
> Stands at a guard with envy; scarce confesses
> That her blood flows, or that her appetite
> Is more to bread than stone: hence shall we see,
> If power change purpose, what our seemers be.

Exeunt.

Scene Three: The Courtroom

Justice, **Pompey**, **Mistress Overdone** *and* **Lucio**. **Mistress Overdone** *and* **Pompey** *await trial.* **Pompey** *is defending them.*

Mistress Overdone

> I am as well acquainted in this court as I was in our house of profession. One would think it were our own house, for here be many of our old customers.

Lucio

You have not heard of the proclamation, have you?

Mistress Overdone

What proclamation, man?

Lucio

All brothel-houses in the suburbs of Vienna must be
plucked down.

Mistress Overdone

What?

Pompey

To the ground, mistress.

Enter **Escalus**, **Isabel** *and the* **Provost**.

Justice

Your honours, these two are accused of keeping a house
of profession, a brothel-house, with many customers.

Escalus

Where were you born?

Pompey

Here in Vienna, sir.

Escalus

What trade are you of in Vienna?

Lucio

She is a tapster, this poor widow's tapster, in her alehouse.
I beseech you, sir, look in this face. Doth your honour
mark her face?

Escalus

Ay, sir, very well.

Lucio

Doth your honour see any harm in this face?

Escalus

Why, no.

Lucio

And her face is the worst thing about her.

Isabel

Your name, mistress?

Mistress Overdone

Mistress Overdone.

Isabel

Have you had any more than one husband?

Pompey

Nine, madam: Overdone by the last.

Isabel

This will last out a night in Russia
When nights are longest there. I'll take my leave,
And leave you to the hearing of the cause,
Hoping you'll find a good cause to whip them both.

Exit **Isabel**.

Escalus

Come hither to me, Mistress Tapster. What's your name,
Mistress Tapster?

Pompey

Pompey.

Escalus

What else?

Pompey

Truly, sir, I am a poor woman that would live.

Escalus

How would you live, Pompey? By being a bawd? What do
you think of the trade, Pompey? Is it a lawful trade?

Pompey

If the law would allow it, sir.

Escalus

But the law will not allow it, Pompey; nor it shall not be allowed in Vienna.

Lucio

Does your worship mean to geld and splay all the youth of the city?

Escalus

No, Lucio.

Lucio

Truly, sir, in my poor opinion, they will to't then. If your worship will take order for the drabs and the knaves, you need not to fear the bawds.

Escalus

There are pretty orders beginning, I can tell you: it is but heading and hanging.

Lucio

If you head and hang all that offend that way, you'll have to give out a commission for more heads: if this law hold in Vienna ten year, I'll rent the fairest house for three-pence a week: if you live to see this come to pass, say I told you so.

Escalus

Thank you, good Lucio; and, in requital of your prophecy, hark you: I advise you, let me not find these two before me again upon any complaint whatsoever; no, not for dwelling where they do: if I do, Lucio, and, in plain dealing, I shall have them both whipped.

Lucio

They thank your worship for your good counsel.

Exit **Escalus** *and* **Justice**. *Enter* **Claudio** *and* **Provost**.

Pompey

Whip me? No, the valiant heart is not whipped out of her trade.

Mistress Overdone

Why, here's a change indeed in the commonwealth! What shall become of me?

Pompey

Come; fear you not: good counsellors lack no clients: though you change your place, you need not change your trade. Courage, there will be pity taken on you, you that have almost work your eyes out in the service. You will be considered.

Mistress Overdone

Well, well; here's one arrested was worth five thousand of us.

Lucio

Who's that?

Mistress Overdone

Claudio.

Lucio

What has he done?

Pompey

A woman.

Lucio

Pray, what's his offence?

Pompey

Groping for trouts in a peculiar river.

Lucio

Why, how now, Claudio! whence comes this restraint?

Mistress Overdone

Let's withdraw.

Exit **Mistress Overdone** *and* **Pompey**.

Claudio

From too much liberty, my Lucio, liberty.

Lucio

What's thy offence, Claudio?

Claudio

What but to speak of would offend again.

Lucio

Is't murder?

Claudio

        No.

Lucio

             Lechery?

Claudio

                  Call it so.

Thus stands it with me: upon a true contract
I got possession of Julietta's bed:
You know the lady; she is fast my wife,
Only for propagation of a dowry
Remaining in the coffer of her friends,
From whom we thought it meet to hide our love
Till time had made them for us. But it chances
The stealth of our most mutual entertainment
With character too gross is writ on Juliet.

Lucio

With child, perhaps?

Enter **Isabel**, **Escalus** *and* **Justice**.

Claudio

Unhappily, even so. The body public is
A horse whereon this Isabel doth ride,
Who, newly in the seat, that it may know
She can command, lets it straight feel her spur.
This new judge awakes me all the penalties
Which have, like unscour'd armour, hung by the wall
So long that fourteen zodiacs have gone round
And none of them been worn; and, for a name,
Now puts the drowsy and neglected act
Freshly on me: 'tis surely for a name.

Lucio

> I warrant it is. Send after the duke and appeal
> to him.

Claudio

> I have done so, but he's not to be found.
> I prithee, Lucio, do me this kind service:
> This day my brother should the cloister enter.
> Acquaint him with the danger of my state:
> Implore him, in my voice, that he make friends
> To the strict deputy; for in his youth
> There is a prone and speechless dialect,
> Such as moves women; and well he can persuade.

Lucio

> I'll to him.

Claudio

> 　　　　　I thank you, good friend Lucio.

Lucio

> Within two hours.

Exit **Lucio**.

Isabel

> 　　　　　Where is the prisoner?

Provost

> He is here, if it like your honour.

Escalus

> Let us be keen, and rather cut a little,
> Than fall, and bruise to death. Alas, this gentleman
> Whom I would save, had a most noble father!
> Have we not all, at sometime in our lives
> Err'd in this point which now you censure him,
> And pulled the law upon us.

Isabel

> 'Tis one thing to be tempted, Escalus,
> Another thing to fall: what knows the laws

That thieves do pass on thieves?
When I, that censure him, do so offend,
Let mine own judgment pattern out my death,
And nothing come in partial. Sir, he must die.

Escalus
Be it as your wisdom will.

Isabel
Claudio, you are to be executed:
Let it be by nine to-morrow morning.
Bring him his confessor, let him be prepared.

Exit **Justice** *and* **Claudio**.

Provost
I crave your honour's pardon.
What shall be done, with the groaning Juliet?
She's very near her hour.

Isabel
                    Dispose of her
To some more fitter place, and that with speed.
Let her have needful, but not lavish, means.

Exit **Isabel**.

Escalus
What's a clock, think you?

Provost
Eleven, sir.

Escalus
I pray you, home to dinner with me.

Provost
I humbly thank you.

Escalus
It grieves me for the death of Claudio,
But there's no remedy.

Provost

Judge Isabel is severe.

Escalus

It is but needful.
But yet, poor Claudio. Come sir.

Exeunt **Escalus** *and* **Provost**.

Scene Four: The Retreat

Enter **Angelo** *and* **Francisca**.

Angelo

And has the order no farther privileges?

Francisca

Are not these large enough?

Angelo

Yes, truly; I speak not as desiring more;
But rather wishing a more strict restraint.

Lucio (*without*)

Ho! Peace be in this place!

Angelo

Who's that which calls?

Francisca

Turn you the key, and know his business of him;
You may, I may not; you are yet unsworn.
If I speak I must not show my face,
Or if I show my face, I must not speak.

Exit **Francisca**.

Angelo

Peace and prosperity! Who is't that calls?

Enter **Lucio**.

Lucio

Can you bring me to the sight of Angelo,
Brother to the unhappy Claudio.

Angelo

I am that Angelo and his brother.

Lucio

Gentle youth, your brother kindly greets you:
Not to be weary with you, he's in prison.

Angelo

For what?

Lucio

For that which, if myself might be his judge,
He should receive his punishment in thanks:
He hath got his friend with child.

Angelo

Sir, make me not your story.

Lucio

It is true.
I hold you as a thing ensky'd and sainted.
By your renouncement an immortal spirit,
And to be talk'd with in sincerity.

Angelo

You do blaspheme the good in mocking me.

Lucio

Do not believe it. Fewness and truth, 'tis thus:
Your brother and his lover have embraced.

Angelo

Some one with child by him? My cousin Juliet?

Lucio

Your cousin?

Angelo

Adoptedly.

Lucio

She it is.

Angelo

O, let him marry her.

Lucio

This is the point.
The duke is very strangely gone from hence;
And with full line of his authority,
Governs Isabel; a woman whose blood
Is very snow-broth; one who never feels.
Giving fear to liberty, she picked out an act,
Under whose heavy sense your brother's life
Falls into forfeit: she arrests him on it;
And follows close the letter of the law,
To make him an example. All hope is gone,
Unless you have the grace by your fair prayer
To soften Isabel.

Angelo

Doth she so seek his life?

Lucio

The provost hath
A warrant for his execution.

Angelo

Alas! what poor ability's in me
To do him good?

Lucio

Try the power you have.

Angelo

My power? Alas, I doubt –

Lucio

Our doubts are traitors
And make us lose the good we oft might win
By fearing to attempt. When young ones kneel
Men give like gods.

Angelo

> I'll see what I can do.

Lucio

But speedily.

Angelo

I will about it straight;
No longer staying but to give Francisca
Notice of my affair. I humbly thank you.

Lucio

I take my leave of you.

Angelo

> Good sir, adieu.

Exeunt.

Act Two

Scene One: The Courtroom

Enter **Isabel** *and* **Provost**.

Isabel
Now, what's the matter. Provost?

Provost
Is it your will Claudio shall die tomorrow?

Isabel
Did not I tell thee yea? Hadst thou not order?
Why dost thou ask again?

Provost
                              Lest I might be too rash:
Under your good correction, I have seen,
When, after execution, judgment hath
Repented o.'er her doom.

Isabel
Do you your office, or give up your place.

Provost
Here is the brother of the man condemn'd
Desires access to you.

Isabel
                              Hath he a brother?

Provost
Ay, my good lady.

Isabel
Well, let him be admitted.

Exit **Provost**.

Re-enter **Provost** *wth* **Angelo** *and* **Lucio**.

Provost
God save your honour!

Isabel (*to* **Provost**)

                  Stay a little while.

(*To* **Angelo**.) You're welcome: what's your will?

Angelo

    I am a woeful suitor to your honour,

    Please but your honour hear me.

Isabel

                  Well, what's your suit?

Angelo

    There is a vice that most I do abhor,

    And most desire should meet the blow of justice;

    For which I would not plead, but that I must;

    For which I must not plead, but that I am

    At war 'twixt will and will not.

Isabel

                  Well, the matter?

Angelo

    I have a brother is condemn'd to die:

    I do beseech you, let it be his fault,

    And not my brother.

Provost (*aside*)

    Heaven give thee moving graces!

Angelo

    Must he needs die?

Isabel

             Youth, there's no remedy.

Angelo

    I had a brother, then. Heaven keep your honour!

Lucio (*aside to* **Angelo**)

    Give't not o'er so: to her again, entreat her;

    Kneel down before her. You are too cold.

Angelo

Yet I do think that you might pardon him,
And neither heaven nor man grieve at the mercy.

Isabel

I will not do't.

Angelo

But can you, if you would?

Isabel

Look, what I will not, that I cannot do.

Angelo

But might you do't, and do the world no wrong,
If so your heart were touch'd with that remorse
As mine is to him?

Isabel

He's sentenced; 'tis too late.

Lucio (*aside to* **Angelo**)

You are too cold.

Angelo

Too late? why, no; I, that do speak a word.
May call it back again. Well, believe this,
No ceremony that to great ones 'longs,
Not the king's crown, nor the deputed sword,
The marshal's truncheon, nor the judge's robe,
Become them with one half so good a grace
As mercy does.

Isabel

Pray you, be gone.

Angelo

I would to heaven I had your potency,
And you were Angelo! Should it then be thus?
No: I would tell what 'twere to be a judge,
And what a prisoner.

Lucio (*aside to* **Angelo**)
Ay, touch her; there's the vein.

Isabel
Your brother is a forfeit of the law,
And you but waste your words.

Angelo
                           Alas, alas!
Why, all the souls that were were forfeit once.

Isabel
It is the law, not I condemn your brother:
Were he my kinsman, brother, or my son,
It should be thus with him: he must die tomorrow.

Angelo
To-morrow! O, that's sudden! Spare him, spare him!
He's not prepared for death. Even for our kitchens
We kill the fowl of season: bethink you;
Who is it that hath died for this offence?
There's many have committed it.

Lucio (*aside to* **Angelo**)
Ay, well said.

Isabel
The law hath not been dead, though it hath slept:
Now 'tis awake, takes note of what is done,
And like a prophet, looks in a glass
That shows what future evils to be hatched and born
Are now to have no successive degrees,
But here they live to end.

Angelo
                        Yet show some pity.

Isabel
I show it most of all when I show justice;
For then I pity those I do not know.
Your brother dies to-morrow; be content.

Angelo

So you must be the first that gives this sentence,
And he, that suffers. O, it is excellent
To have a giant's strength; but it is tyrannous
To use it like a giant.

Lucio (*aside to* **Angelo**)

That's well said.

Angelo

Could great ones thunder
As Jove himself does, Jove would ne'er be quiet,
For every pelting, petty officer
Would use his heaven for thunder;
Nothing but thunder! But man, proud man,
Dressed in a little brief authority,
Most ignorant of what he's most assured,
His glassy essence, like an angry ape,
Plays such fantastic tricks before high heaven
As make the angels weep.

Lucio (*aside to* **Angelo**)

O, to her, to her, boy! She will relent; she's coming;
I perceive 't.

Angelo

We cannot weigh our brother with ourself:
Great men may jest with saints; 'tis wit in them,
But in the less foul profanation.

Lucio

More of that, youth.

Angelo

Go to your bosom;
Knock there, and ask your heart what it doth know
That's like my brother's fault: if it confess
A natural guiltiness such as is his,
Let it not sound a thought upon your tongue
Against my brother's life.

Isabel (*aside*)
> He speaks, and 'tis
> Such sense, that my sense breeds with it.
> (*To* **Angelo**.) Fare you well.

Angelo
> Gentle judge, turn back.

Isabel
> Come again tomorrow.

Angelo
> Hark how I'll bribe you: your honour, turn back.

Isabel
> How! Bribe me?

Angelo
> Ay, with such gifts that heaven shall share with you.

Lucio (*aside to* **Angelo**)
> You had marr'd all else.

Angelo
> Not with tested gold; but with true prayers
> That shall fly up to heaven and enter there
> Ere sun-rise. Prayers from a fasting soul.

Isabel
> Well; come to me to-morrow.

Lucio (*aside to* **Angelo**)
> Go to; 'tis well: away!

Angelo
> Heaven keep your honour safe!

Isabel
>   Amen.
> (*Aside.*) For I am that way going to temptation,
> Where prayers cross.

Angelo

                        At what hour to-morrow
  Shall I attend your honour?

Isabel

  At any time 'fore noon.

Angelo

  'Save your honour!

Exeunt **Angelo**, **Lucio** *and* **Provost**.

Isabel

  From thee, even from thy virtue!
  What's this, what's this? Is this his fault or mine?
  The tempter or the tempted, who sins most?
  Ha! Can it be? Having waste ground enough,
  Shall we desire to raze the sanctuary
  And pitch our evils there? O, fie, fie, fie!
  What dost thou, or what art thou, Isabel?
  Dost thou desire him foully for those things
  That make him good? O, let his brother live!
  Thieves for their robbery have authority
  When judges steal themselves. What, do I love him,
  That I desire to hear him speak again,
  And feast upon his eyes? What is't I dream on?
  O cunning enemy, that, to catch a saint,
  With saints dost bait thy hook! Most dangerous
  Is that temptation that doth goad us on
  To sin in loving virtue. Even till now,
  When men were fond, I smiled and wonder'd how.

Exit **Isabel**.

Scene Two: The Prison

Duke, *disguised as before, and the* **Provost**.

Duke

  Hail to you, Provost! So I think you are.

Provost

I am the provost. What's your will, good friar?

Duke

Bound by my charity and my blest order,
I come to visit the afflicted spirits
Here in the prison. Do me the common right
To let me see them.

Provost

I would do more than that, if more were needful.

Enter **Claudio**.

Duke

When must he die?

Provost

As I do think, tomorrow.

Duke

Is there a hope of pardon?

Claudio

The miserable have no other medicine
But only hope:
I've hope to live, and am prepared to die.

Duke

Be absolute for death; either death or life
Shall thereby be the sweeter. Reason thus with life:
If I do lose thee, I do lose a thing
That none but fools would keep: a breath thou art,
Servile to all the skyey influences,
That dost this habitation, where thou keep'st,
Hourly afflict: merely, thou art death's fool;
For him thou labour'st by thy flight to shun
And yet runn'st toward him still. Thy best of rest is sleep,
And that thou oft provokest; yet grossly fear'st
Thy death, which is no more. Thou art not thyself;
For thou exist'st on many a thousand grains
That issue out of dust. Happy thou art not;

For what thou hast not, still thou strivest to get,
And what thou hast, forget'st. Thou hast nor youth nor
   age,
But, as it were, an after-dinner's sleep,
Dreaming on both; for all thy blessed youth
Becomes as aged, and doth beg the alms
Of palsied eld; and when thou art old and rich,
Thou hast neither heat, affection, limb, nor beauty,
To make thy riches pleasant. What's yet in this
That bears the name of life? Yet in this life
Lie hid more thousand deaths: yet death we fear,
That makes these odds all even.

Claudio

I humbly thank you.
To sue to live, I find I seek to die;
And, seeking death, find life: let it come on.

Exeunt.

Scene Three: The Courtroom

Enter **Isabel**.

Isabel
When I would pray and think, I think and pray
To several subjects. Heaven hath my empty words;
Whilst my invention, hearing not my tongue,
Anchors on Angelo: Heaven in my mouth,
As if I did but only chew his name;
And in my heart the strong and swelling evil
Of my conception. O place, O form,
How often dost thou with thy case, thy habit,
Wrench awe from fools and tie the wiser souls
To thy false seeming! Blood, thou art blood.

Enter **Provost**.

How now! who's there?

Provost

One Angelo desires access to you.

Isabel

Teach him the way.

Exit **Provost**.

O heavens!
Why does my blood thus muster to my heart,
Making both it unable for itself,
And dispossessing all my other parts
Of necessary fitness?
So play the foolish throngs with one that swoons;
Come all to help her, and so stop the air
By which she should revive.

Enter **Angelo**.

How now, fair youth?

Angelo

I am come to know your pleasure.

Isabel

That you might know it, would much better please me
Than to demand what 'tis. Your brother cannot live.

Angelo

Even so. Heaven keep your honour!

Isabel

Yet may he live awhile; and, it may be,
As long as you or I yet he must die.

Angelo

Under your sentence?

Isabel

Yea.

Angelo

When, I beseech you?

Isabel

Ha! fie, these filthy vices! It were as good
To pardon him that hath from nature stolen
A man already made, as to remit
His saucy sweetness, that do coin heaven's image
In stamps that are forbid.

Angelo

'Tis set down so in heaven, but not in earth.

Isabel

Say you so? then I shall pose you quickly.
Which had you rather, that the most just law
Now took your brother's life; or, to redeem him,
Give up your body to such sweet uncleanness
As Juliet that he hath stain'd?

Angelo

Madam, believe this,
I had rather give my body than my soul.

Isabel

I talk not of your soul.

Angelo

How say you?

Isabel

I, now the voice of the recorded law,
Pronounce a sentence on your brother's life:
Might there not be a charity in sin
To save this brother's life?

Angelo

Please you to do't,
I'll take it as a peril to my soul,
It is no sin at all, but charity.

Isabel

Pleased you to do't at peril of your soul,
Were equal poise of sin and charity.

Angelo

That I do beg his life, if it be sin,
Heaven let me bear it! Your granting of my suit,
If that be sin, I'll make it my morn prayer
To have it added to the faults of mine,
And nothing of your answer.

Isabel

                              Nay, but hear me.
Your sense pursues not mine: either you are ignorant,
Or seem so craftily; and that's not good.
To be received plain, I'll speak more gross:
Your brother is to die.

Angelo

So.

Isabel

And his offence is so, as it appears,
Accountant to the law upon that pain.

Angelo

True.

Isabel

What should happen if that you, his brother,
Finding yourself desired of such a person,
Whose credit with the judge, or own great place,
Could fetch your brother from the manacles
Of the all-binding law; and that there were
No earthly mean to save him, but that either
You must lay down the treasures of your body
To this supposed, or else to let him suffer;
What would you do?

Angelo

As much for my poor brother as myself:
That is, were I under the terms of death,
The impression of keen whips I'd wear as rubies,
And strip myself to death, as to a bed
That longing have been sick for, ere I'd yield
My body up to shame.

Isabel

Then must your brother die.

Angelo

And 'twere the cheaper way:
Better it were a brother died at once,
Than that a brother, by redeeming him,
Should die for ever.

Isabel

Were not you then as cruel as the sentence
That you have slander'd so?

Angelo

Ignomy in ransom and free pardon
Are of two houses: lawful mercy
Is nothing kin to foul redemption.

Isabel

You seem'd of late to make the law a tyrant;
And rather proved the sliding of your brother
A merriment than a vice.

Angelo

O, pardon me, good judge; it oft falls out,
To have what we would have, we speak not what we
mean:
I something do excuse the thing I hate,
For his advantage that I dearly love.

Isabel

We are all frail.

Angelo

Men are frail too.

Isabel

I think it well:
Since I suppose we are made to be no stronger
Than faults may shake our frames, let me be bold;
I do arrest your words. Be that you are,
That is, a man; if you be more, you're none;

If you be one, as you are well express'd
By all external warrants, show it now,
By putting on the destined livery.

Angelo

I have no tongue but one: gentle madam,
Let me entreat you speak the former language.

Isabel

Plainly conceive, I love you.

Angelo

My brother did love Juliet,
And you tell me that he shall die for it.

Isabel

He shall not, Angelo, if you give me love.

Angelo

I know your virtue hath a licence in't,
Which seems a little fouler than it is,
To pluck on others.

Isabel

                Believe me, on mine honour,
My words express my purpose.

Angelo

Ha! little honour to be much believed,
And most pernicious purpose! Seeming, seeming!
I will proclaim thee, Isabel; look for't:
Sign me a present pardon for my brother,
Or with an outstretch'd throat I'll tell the world aloud
What thou art.

Isabel

                Who will believe thee, Angelo?
My unsoil'd name, the austereness of my life,
My vouch against you, and my place i' the state,
Will so your accusation overweigh,
That you shall stifle in your own report
And smell of calumny. I have begun,

And now I give my sensual race the rein:
Fit thy consent to my sharp appetite;
By yielding up thy body to my will;
Or else your brother must not only die,
But thy unkindness shall his death draw out
To lingering sufferance. Answer me to-morrow,
Or, by the affection that now guides me most,
I'll prove a tyrant to him. As for you,
Say what you can, my false o'erweighs your true.

Exit **Isabel**.

Angelo
To whom should I complain? Did I tell this,
Who would believe me? I'll to my brother:
Though he hath fallen by prompture of the blood,
Yet hath he in him such a mind of honour
That, had he twenty heads to tender down
On twenty bloody blocks, he'd yield them up,
Before his brother should his body stoop
To such abhorr'd pollution.
Then, Angelo, live chaste, and, brother, die:
More than our brother is our chastity.
I'll tell him yet of Isabel's request,
And fit his mind to death, for his soul's rest.

Exit **Angelo**.

Act Three

Scene One: The Prison

Enter **Angelo** *to greet the* **Provost** *as the* **Duke**, *disguised as before, leaves* **Claudio**.

Angelo
Peace here; grace and good company!

Provost
Who's there?

Duke
Dear sir, ere long I'll visit you again.

Angelo
My business is a word or two with Claudio.

Claudio
Most holy sir, I thank you.

Provost
And very welcome. Look, signior, here's your brother.

Duke
Provost, a word with you.

Provost
As many as you please.

Duke
Bring me to hear them speak, where I may be concealed.

Exeunt **Duke** *and* **Provost**.

Claudio
Now, brother, what's the comfort?

Angelo
Why, as all comforts are; most good, most good indeed.
This Isabel, having affairs to heaven,
Intends you for her swift ambassador,
Therefore your best appointment make with speed;
To-morrow you set on.

Claudio

Is there no remedy?

Angelo

None, but such remedy as, to save a head,
To cleave a heart in twain.

Claudio

But is there any?

Angelo

Yes, brother, you may live:
There is a devilish mercy in the judge,
If you'll implore it, that will free your life,
But fetter you till death.

Claudio

But in what nature?

Angelo

In such a one as, you consenting to't,
Would bark your honour from that trunk you bear,
And leave you naked.

Claudio

Let me know the point.

Angelo

O, I do fear thee, Claudio; Darest thou die?
The sense of death is most in apprehension;
And the poor beetle, that we tread upon,
In corporal sufferance finds a pang as great
As when a giant dies.

Claudio

Why give you me this shame?
Think you I can a resolution fetch
From flowery tenderness? If I must die,
I will encounter darkness as a bride,
And hug it in mine arms.

Angelo

There spake my brother; there my father's grave
Did utter forth a voice. Yes, thou must die:
Thou art too noble to conserve a life
In base cowardice. This outward-sainted deputy,
Whose settled visage and deliberate word
Nips youth i' the head, is yet a devil.
Her filth within being cast, she would appear
A pond as deep as hell.

Claudio

The pious Isabel!

Angelo

If I would yield her my virginity,
Thou mightst be freed.

Claudio

O heavens! it cannot be.

Angelo

O, were it but my life,
I'd throw it down for your deliverance
As frankly as a pin.

Claudio

Thanks, dear Angelo.

Angelo

Be ready, Claudio, for your death tomorrow.

Claudio

Yes. Has she affections in her?
Sure, it is no sin,
Or of the deadly seven, it is the least.

Angelo

Which is the least?

Claudio

O Angelo!

Angelo
What says my brother?

Claudio
                              Death is a fearful thing.

Angelo
And shamed life a hateful.

Claudio
Ay, but to die, and go we know not where;
To lie in cold obstruction and to rot;
This sensible warm motion to become
A kneaded clod; and the delighted spirit
To bathe in fiery floods, or to reside
In thrilling region of thick-ribbed ice;
To be imprison'd in the viewless winds,
And blown with restless violence round about
The pendent world; or to be worse than worst
Of those that lawless and incertain thought
Imagine howling: 'tis too horrible!
The weariest and most loathed worldly life
That age, ache, penury and imprisonment
Can lay on nature is a paradise
To what we fear of death.

Angelo
Alas, alas!

Claudio
           Sweet brother, let me live:
What sin you do to save Claudio's life,
Nature dispenses with the deed so far
That it becomes a virtue.

Angelo
                         O faithless coward!
Wilt thou be made a man out of my vice?
Is't not a kind of incest, to take life
From thine own brother's shame? What should I think?
Die, perish! Might but my bending down

Reprieve thee from thy fate, it should proceed:
I'll pray a thousand prayers for thy death,
No word to save thee.

Claudio

Nay, hear me, Angelo.

Angelo

O, fie, fie, fie!
Thy sin's not accidental, but a trade.
Mercy to thee would prove itself a bawd:
'Tis best thou diest quickly.

Claudio

O hear me, Angelo!

Re-enter **Duke**.

Duke

Vouchsafe a word, young brother, but one word.

Angelo

What is your will?

Duke

Might you dispense with your leisure, I would by and by
have some speech with you: the satisfaction I would
require is likewise your own benefit.

Angelo

I have no superfluous leisure; my stay must be stolen out
of other affairs; but I will attend you awhile.

Exit **Angelo**.

Duke

Son, I have overheard what hath passed between you and
your brother. Isabel had never the purpose to corrupt
him; only she hath made a trial of his virtue. I am
confessor to Isabel, and I know this to be true; therefore
prepare yourself to death: go to your knees and make
ready.

Claudio

Let me ask my brother pardon. I am so out of love with life that I will pray to be rid of it.

Duke

Hold you there: farewell.

Exit **Claudio**.

Provost, a word with you!

Re-enter **Provost**.

Provost

What's your will, father?

Duke

That now you are come, you will be gone. Leave me awhile with the youth: no loss shall touch him by my company.

Provost

In good time.

Exit **Provost**. *Enter* **Angelo**.

Duke

The assault that Isabel hath made to you, fortune hath conveyed to my understanding. She made trial of you only. Therefore fasten your ear on my advisings: to the love I have in doing good, a remedy presents itself. I do make myself believe that you may most do a poor wronged man a merited benefit; redeem your brother from the angry law; do no stain to your own gracious person; and much please the absent duke, if peradventure he shall ever return to have hearing of this business.

Angelo

Let me hear you speak farther. I have spirit to do anything that appears not foul in the truth of my spirit.

Duke

Virtue is bold, and goodness never fearful. Have you not heard speak of Frederick the merchant, whose cargo, some five years since, miscarried at sea?

Angelo

I have heard of the fellow, and good words went with his name.

Duke

He should this Isabel have married; was bound to her by oath, and the nuptial appointed. Between which time, this Frederick lost his ship and with it all his fortune.

Angelo

Can this be so? Did Isabel so leave him?

Duke

Left him in tears, and dried not one of them with her comfort; swallowed her vows whole, pretending in him discoveries of dishonour: and she, a marble to his tears, is washed with them, but relents not.

Angelo

What corruption in this life, that it will let this woman live!

Duke

The cure of this not only saves your brother, but keeps you from dishonour.

Angelo

Show me how, good father.

Duke

This Frederick hath yet in him the continuance of his first affection. Her unjust unkindness, that in all reason should have quenched his love, hath, like an impediment in the current, made it more violent and unruly. Go you to Isabel: answer her requiring with a plausible obedience. Agree with her demands to the point; only that your stay with her may not be long; that the time may have all

shadow and silence in it; and the place answer to
convenience. This being granted (and now follows all) we
shall advise this wronged man to go in your place. Here,
by this, is your brother saved, your honour untainted, the
poor Frederick advantaged, and the corrupt Isabel scaled.
What think you of it?

Angelo

The image of it gives me content already; and I trust it
will grow to a most prosperous perfection.

Duke

It lies much in your holding up. Haste you speedily to
Isabel: if for this night she entreat you to her bed, give
her promise of satisfaction. I will presently to Saint
Luke's. There, at the moated grange, resides this dejected
Frederick. At that place call upon me; and dispatch with
Isabel, that it may be quickly.

Angelo

I thank you for this comfort. Fare you well,
good father.

Exeunt.

Scene Two: The Prison

Duke, *disguised as before, the* **Justice** *with* **Pompey**.

Justice

Come your way, madam. 'Bless you, good friar.

Duke

And you. What offence hath this woman made you, sir?

Justice

Marry, sir she hath offended the law, that she still needs
buy and sell men and women like beasts.

Duke

Canst thou believe thy living is a life, so stinkingly
depending? Go mend, go mend.

Pompey

Indeed, it does stink in some sort, sir; but yet, sir, I would
prove –

Duke

Take her to prison, officer.

Justice

She must before the deputy, sir; she has given her
warning: the deputy cannot abide a whoremaster.

Enter **Lucio**.

Pompey

I spy comfort; I cry bail. Here's a friend of mine.

Lucio

How now, noble Pompey! What, at the wheels of Caesar?
What reply, ha? Is the world as it was, man? Which is the
way? Is it sad, and few words? Or how? The trick of it? Art
going to prison, Pompey?

Pompey

Yes, faith, sir.

Lucio

For debt Pompey or how?

Pompey

For being a bawd, for being a bawd.

Lucio

Why, 'tis not amiss, Pompey. Farewell.

Pompey

I hope, sir, your good worship will be my bail.

Lucio

No, indeed, will I not, Pompey. Adieu, trusty Pompey.
'Bless you, friar.

Duke
And you.

Provost
Come your ways, sir; come.

Pompey
You will not bail me, then, sir?

Lucio
Go to kennel, Pompey; go.

Exeunt **Pompey** *and* **Justice**.

What news, friar, of the duke?

Duke
I know none. Can you tell me of any?

Lucio
It was a mad fantastical trick of him to steal from the state, and usurp the beggary he was never born to. Judge Isabel dukes it well in his absence.

Duke
She does well in 't.

Lucio
A little more lenity to lechery would do no harm in her, friar.

Duke
It is too general a vice, and severity must cure it.

Lucio
They say this Isabel was not made by man and woman: is it true, think you?

Duke
How should she be made, then?

Lucio
Some report a sea-maid spawned her; some, that she was begot between two stock-fishes. But it is certain that when she makes water her urine is congealed ice; that I know to be true.

Duke

You are pleasant, sir.

Lucio

Why, what a ruthless thing is this in her, for the rebellion of a codpiece to take away the life of a man! Would the duke that is absent have done this? Ere he would have hanged a man for the getting a hundred bastards, he would have paid for the nursing a thousand: he had some feeling of the sport: he knew the service, and that instructed him to mercy.

Duke

I never heard the absent duke much detected for women; he was not inclined that way.

Lucio

O, sir, you are deceived.

Duke

'Tis not possible.

Lucio

Who, not the duke? Yes, a fifty year old beggar; and his use was to put a ducat in her clack-dish. He would be drunk too; that let me inform you.

Duke

Either this is the envy in you, folly, or mistaking. Let him be but testimonied, and he shall appear to the envious a scholar, a statesman and a soldier.

Lucio

Sir, I know him, and I love him.

Duke

Love talks with better knowledge, and knowledge with dearer love.

Lucio

Come, sir, I know what I know.

Duke

I can hardly believe that, since you know not what you speak. I pray you, your name?

Lucio

Sir, my name is Lucio; well known to the duke.

Duke

He shall know you better, sir, if I may live to report you.

Lucio

I fear you not. But no more of this. Canst thou tell if Claudio die to-morrow or no?

Duke

Why should he die, sir?

Lucio

Why? For filling a bottle with a tundish. I would the duke we talk of were returned again: the ungenitured deputy will unpeople the province with her continency; sparrows must not build in her house-eaves, because they are lecherous. The duke yet would have dark deeds darkly answered; he would never bring them to light: would he were returned! Marry, this Claudio is condemned for untrussing. Farewell, good friar: I prithee, pray for me. The duke, I say to thee again, would mouth with a beggar, though she smelt brown bread and garlic: say that I said so. Farewell.

Exit **Lucio**.

Duke

Back-wounding calumny.

Enter **Escalus** *and* **Provost**, *with* **Mistress Overdone**.

Escalus

What? Before me again?

Mistress Overdone

Good my lord, be good to me; your honour is accounted a merciful man; good my lord.

Provost

A bawd of eleven years continuance, may it please your
honour.

Mistress Overdone

My lord, this is one Lucio's information against me.
Mistress Kate Keepdown was with child by him in the
duke's time, he promised her marriage, his child is a year
and a quarter old – I have kept it myself – and see how he
goes about to abuse me.

Escalus

That fellow is a fellow of much licence, let him be called
before us. Away with her to prison! Go to; no more words.
Provost, Isabel will not be altered; Claudio must die to-
morrow: let him be furnished with divines, and have all
charitable preparation.

Provost

So please you, this friar hath been with him, and advised
him for the entertainment of death.

Exeunt **Provost** *with* **Mistress Overdone**.

Escalus

Good even, good father.

Duke

Bliss and goodness on you!

Escalus

What news abroad i' the world?

Duke

None, but that there is so great a fever on goodness, that
the dissolution of it must cure it. This news is old enough,
yet it is every day's news. I pray you, sir, of what
disposition was the duke?

Escalus

One that, above all other strifes, contended especially to
know himself.

Duke

What pleasure was he given to?

Escalus

A gentleman of all temperance. But leave we him to his events, with a prayer they may prove prosperous; and let me desire to know how you find Claudio prepared. I am made to understand that you have lent him visitation.

Duke

He most willingly humbles himself to the determination of justice, and is resolved to die.

Escalus

I have laboured for the poor gentleman to the extremest shore of my modesty: but my sister justice have I found so severe, that she hath forced me to tell her she is indeed Justice.

Duke

If her own life answer the straitness of her proceeding, it shall become her well; wherein if she chance to fail, she hath sentenced herself.

Escalus

I am going to visit the prisoner. Fare you well.

Duke

Peace be with you!

Exeunt.

Act Four

Scene One: The Retreat

Enter **Frederick** *and* **Thomas**.

A song:

> Take oh, take those lips away,
> That so sweetly were forsworn;
> And those eyes, the break of day,
> Lights that do mislead the morn:
> But my kisses bring again, bring again;
> Seals of love, but sealed in vain, sealed in vain.

Enter **Duke**, *disguised as before*.

Thomas
 Let me excuse me.

Duke
 I cry you mercy, sir.

Exit **Thomas**.

 I pray, you, tell me, hath any body inquired for me here
 to-day? Much upon this time have I promised here to
 meet.

Frederick
 You have not been inquired after: I have sat here all day.

Enter **Angelo**.

Duke
 I do constantly believe you. The time is come even now. I
 shall crave your forbearance a little: may be I will call
 upon you anon, for some advantage to yourself.

Frederick
 I am always bound to you.

Exit **Frederick**.

Duke

Very well met, and well come.
What is the news from this good deputy?

Angelo

She hath a garden walled in with brick,
That makes his opening with this little key:
There have I made my promise
Upon the heavy middle of the night.
I have possess'd her my most stay
Can be but brief; for I have made her know
I have a servant comes with me along,
That stays upon me, whose persuasion is
I come about my brother.

Duke

'Tis well borne up.
I have not yet made known to Frederick
A word of this. What, ho! within! come forth!

Re-enter **Frederick**.

I pray you, be acquainted with this youth;
He comes to do you good.

Frederick

I do desire the like.

Duke

Do you persuade yourself that I respect you?

Frederick

Good friar, I know you do, and have found it.

Duke

Take, then, this your companion by the hand,
Who hath a story ready for your ear.
I shall attend your leisure: but make haste;
The vaporous night approaches.

Frederick

Will't please you walk aside?

Exeunt **Frederick** *and* **Angelo**.

Duke

O place and greatness! millions of false eyes
Are stuck upon thee: volumes of report
Run with these false and most contrarious quests
Upon thy doings: thousand escapes of wit
Make thee the father of their idle dreams
And rack thee in their fancies.

Re-enter **Frederick** *and* **Angelo**.

Welcome, how agreed?

Angelo

He'll take the enterprise upon him, father,
If you advise it.

Duke

It is not only my consent,
But my entreaty too.

Angelo

Little have you to say
When you depart from her, but, soft and low,
'Remember now my brother.'

Frederick

Fear me not.

Duke

Nor, gentle brother, fear you not at all.
She is your wife upon a pre-contract.
To bring you thus together, 'tis no sin.

Exeunt.

Scene Two: The Prison

Enter **Provost** *and* **Duke**, *disguised as before*.

Duke

Good Provost! Who called here of late?

Provost

None, since the curfew rung.

Duke

Not Angelo?

Provost

No.

Duke

He will, then, before long.

Provost

What comfort is for Claudio?

Duke

There's some in hope.

Provost

It is a bitter deputy.

Duke

Not so, not so; her life is parallel'd
Even with the stroke and line of her great justice.
This is Isabel's man.

Exit **Provost**.

And here comes Claudio's pardon.

Re-enter **Provost**.

Now, sir, what news?
Pray you, let's hear.

Provost (*reads*)

'Whatsoever you may hear to the contrary, let Claudio be
executed by four of the clock. Let this be duly performed;
with a thought that more depends on it than we must yet
deliver. Thus fail not to do your office, as you will answer
it at your peril.' What say you to this, sir?

Duke

I will lay myself in hazard. Claudio, whom here you have
warrant to execute, is no greater forfeit to the law than

Isabel who hath sentenced him. To prove this, I crave but
four days' respite; for the which you are to do me both a
present and a dangerous courtesy.

Provost

Pray, sir, in what?

Duke

In the delaying death.

Provost

Alack, how may I do it, having the hour limited, and an
express command, under penalty. Pardon me, good
father; it is against my oath.

Duke

Were you sworn to the duke, or to the deputy?

Provost

To him, and to his substitutes.

Duke

Since I see you fearful, I will go further than I meant.
Look you, sir, here is the hand and seal of the duke: you
know the character, I doubt not; and the signet is not
strange to you.

Provost

I know them both.

Duke

The contents of this is the return of the duke: you shall
find, within these two days he will be here. This is a thing
that Isabel knows not; for she this very day receives letters
of strange tenor; perchance of the duke's death. Look, the
unfolding star calls up the shepherd. Put not yourself into
amazement how these things should be: all difficulties are
but easy when they are known.

Provost

This shall be done, good father, presently.
And how shall we continue Claudio,
To save me from the danger that might come
If he were known alive?

Duke
> Let this be done. Put him in a secret cell.

Provost
> I am your free dependant.

Duke
> Send news of his execution to Isabel.

Provost
> I'll make all speed.

Exit **Provost**.

Angelo (*within*)
> Peace, ho, be here!

Duke
> The tongue of Angelo. He's come to know
> If yet his brother's pardon be come hither:
> But I will keep him ignorant of his good,
> To comfort his despair when least expected.

Enter **Angelo**.

Duke
> Good morning to you, pure and gracious youth.

Angelo
> The better, given me by so holy a man.
> Hath yet the deputy sent my brother's pardon?

Duke
> She hath released him, Angelo, from the world.

Angelo
> Nay, but it is not so.

Duke
> It is no other: show your wisdom, son,
> In your close patience.

Angelo
> O, I will to her and pluck out her eyes!

Duke

You shall not be admitted to her sight.

Angelo

Unhappy Claudio! wretched Angelo!
Injurious world! most damnèd Isabel!

Duke

This nor hurts her nor profits you a jot;
Forbear it therefore; give your cause to heaven.
The duke comes home tomorrow; nay, dry your eyes.
Escalus and Isabel, meet him at the court,
There to give up their power. You shall have revenge.
Tomorrow, then.

Angelo

Direct me, friar.

Duke

This provost here brings you before the duke.
And in the open court, shall you accuse her.
Command these fretting waters from your eyes
With a light heart. Who's here?

Enter **Lucio**.

Lucio

Good even. Friar, where's the provost?

Duke

Not within, sir.

Lucio

O dearest Angelo, I am pale at mine heart to see thine
eyes so red. But they say the duke will be here tomorrow.
By my troth, Angelo, I loved thy brother: if the old
fantastical duke of dark corners had been at home, he had
lived.

Exit **Angelo**.

Duke

Sir, the duke is marvellous little beholding to your
reports.

Lucio

Friar, thou knowest not the duke so well as I do.

Duke

Well, you'll answer this one day. Fare ye well.

Lucio

Nay, tarry; I'll go along with thee. I can tell thee pretty
tales of the duke.

Duke

You have told me too many of him already, sir.

Lucio

I was once before him for getting a wench with child.

Duke

Did you such a thing?

Lucio

Yes, marry, did I but I denied it; they would else have
married me to the rotten whore.

Duke

Sir, your company is fairer than honest. Rest you well.

Lucio

By my troth, I'll go with thee to the lane's end. If bawdy
talk offend you, we'll have very little of it. Nay, friar, I am
a kind of burr; I shall stick.

Exeunt.

Act Five

Scene One: The Courtroom

Enter **Isabel**.

Isabel

    This deed unshapes me quite, makes me unpregnant
    And dull to all proceedings. A deflower'd youth!
    And by an eminent body that enforced
    The law against it! But that his tender shame
    Will not proclaim against his virgin loss,
    How might he tongue me! Yet reason dares him no;
    For my authority bears of a credent bulk,
    That no particular scandal once can touch
    But it confounds the breather. Would yet he had lived!
    Alack, when once our grace we have forgot,
    Nothing goes right: we would, and we would not.

Enter **Escalus**.

Escalus

    Every letter the duke hath writ contradicts the former.

Isabel

    In most uneven and distracted manner. His actions show
    much like to madness.

Escalus

    I guess not.

Isabel

    And why did he demand it proclaimed, an hour before
    his return, that if any crave redress of injustice, they
    should exhibit their petitions here?

Enter **Duke**.

Duke

    My very worthy judges, fairly met!
    Our old and faithful friend, we are glad to see you.

Isabel

Happy return be to your royal grace!

Duke

Many and hearty thankings to you both.
We have made inquiry of you; and we hear
Such goodness of your justice, that our soul
Cannot but yield you forth to public thanks.

Isabel

You make my bonds still greater.

Duke

Give me your hand,
And let the subject see, to make them know
That outward courtesies would fain proclaim
Favours that keep within.

Enter **Angelo** *with* **Justice** *and the* **Provost** *and* **Frederick** *with* **Thomas**.

Provost

Now is your time: speak loud and kneel
before him.

Angelo

Justice, O royal duke! Dishonour not your eye
By throwing it on any other object
Till you have heard me in my true complaint
And given me justice, justice, justice, justice!

Duke

Relate your wrongs; in what? By whom? Be brief.
Here is a worthy judge shall give you justice:
Reveal yourself to her.

Angelo

O worthy duke,
You bid me seek redemption of the devil:
Hear me yourself; for that which I must speak
Must either punish me, not being believed,
Or wring redress from you. Hear me, O hear me, here!

Isabel

My lord, his wits, I fear me, are not firm:
He hath been a suitor to me for his brother
Cut off by course of justice –

Angelo

By course of justice!

Isabel

And he will speak most bitterly and strange.

Angelo

Most strange, but yet most truly, will I speak:
That Isabel's forsworn; is it not strange?
That Isabel's a murderer; is 't not strange?
That Isabel is a violator;
Is it not strange and strange?

Duke

Nay, it is ten times strange.

Angelo

Nay, it is ten times true; for truth is truth
To the end of reckoning.

Duke

Away with him! Poor soul,
He speaks this in the infirmity of sense.

Angelo

O prince, I conjure thee, as thou believest
There is another comfort than this world,
That thou neglect me not, with that opinion
That I am touch'd with madness! 'Tis not impossible
That one may seem as shy, as grave, as just
As Isabel; even so may Isabel
Be an arch-villain.

Duke

Many that are not mad
Have, sure, more lack of reason. What would you say?

Angelo

I am the brother of one Claudio,
Condemn'd upon the act of fornication
To lose his head; condemn'd by Isabel:
I, was sent to by my brother; one Lucio
As then the messenger –

Lucio

That's I, an't like your grace:
I came to him from Claudio, and desired him
To try his gracious fortune with Judge Isabel
For his poor brother's pardon.

Angelo

That's he indeed.

Duke

You were not bid to speak.

Lucio

No, my good lord;
Nor wish'd to hold my peace.

Duke

I wish you now, then;
Pray you, take note of it: and when you have
A business for yourself, pray heaven you then
Be silent.

Lucio

I warrant your honour.

Duke

The warrant's for yourself; take heed to't.

Angelo

This gentleman told somewhat of my tale –

Lucio

Right.

Duke

It may be right; but you are i' the wrong
To speak before your time. Proceed.

Angelo

                                             I went
To this pernicious, villain deputy –

Duke

That's somewhat madly spoken.

Angelo

Pardon it; the phrase is to the matter.

Duke

Mended again. The matter; proceed.

Angelo

In brief, to set the needless process by,
How I persuaded, how I pray'd, and kneel'd,
How she repelled me, and how I replied –
For this was of much length – the vile conclusion
I now begin with grief and shame to utter:
She would not, but by gift of my chaste body
To her violent, intemperate lust,
Release my brother; and, after much debatement,
My brotherly remorse confutes mine honour,
And I did yield to her: but the next morn betimes,
Her purpose done, she sends a warrant
For my poor brother's head.

Duke

                           This is most likely!

Angelo

O, that it were as like as it is true!

Duke

Her integrity stands without blemish.
This imports no reason. Some one hath set you on:
Confess the truth, and say by whose advice
Thou camest here to complain.

Angelo

                           And is this all?
Then, O you blessed ministers above,
Keep me in patience, and with ripen'd time

Unfold the evil which is here wrapt up
In countenance! Heaven shield your grace from woe,
As I, thus wrong'd, hence unbelieved go!

Duke

I know you'd fain be gone. Shall we thus permit
A blasting and a scandalous breath to fall
On her so near us? This needs must be a practise.
Who knew of your intent and coming here?

Angelo

One that I would were here, a Friar.

Duke

A ghostly father, belike. Who knows that Friar?

Lucio

My lord, I know him; I do not like the man
For certain words he spake against your grace.

Duke

Words against me? Let this friar be found.
Do you not smile at this, Isabel?
O heaven, the vanity of wretched fools!
An officer! To prison with him!
In this I'll be impartial; be you judge
Of your own cause.

Frederick

My lord, let me speak.

Duke

                        Another witness?
First, let him show his face, and after speak.

Frederick

Pardon, my lord; I will not show my face
Until my wife does bid me.

Duke

What, are you married?

Frederick

            No, my lord.

Duke

A widower, then?

Frederick

            Neither, my lord.

Duke

Why, you are nothing then?

Frederick

My lord; I do confess I ne'er was married;
And yet I have known my wife; yet my wife
Knows not that ever she knew me.

Lucio

She was drunk then, my lord: it can be no better.

Duke

For the benefit of silence, would thou wert so too!

Lucio

Well, my lord.

Duke

         You say your wife.

Frederick

Why, just, my lord, and that is Isabel,
Who thinks she knows that she ne'er knew my body,
But knows she thinks that she knows Angelo's.

Isabel

This is a strange abuse. Let's see thy face.

Frederick

My wife does bid me; now I will unmask.
(*Unveiling.*) This is that face, thou cruel Isabel,
Which once thou sworest was worth the looking on;
This is the hand which, with a vow'd contract,
Was fast belock'd in thine; this is the body

That took away the match from Angelo,
And did supply thee at thy garden-house
In his imagined person.

Duke

Know you this man?

Lucio

Carnally, he says.

Duke

Sirrah, no more!

Lucio

Enough, my lord.

Isabel

My lord, I must confess I know this man:
And five years since there was some speech of marriage
Betwixt myself and him; which was broke off,
Partly for that his promised proportions
Came short of composition, but in chief
For that his reputation was disvalued
In levity: since which time of five years
I never spake with him, saw him, nor heard from him,
Upon my faith and honour.

Frederick

Noble prince,
As there comes light from heaven and words from breath,
As there is sense in truth and truth in virtue,
I am this woman's husband as strongly
As words could make up vows: and, my good lord,
But Tuesday night last gone in's garden-house
She knew me as a husband.

Isabel

I did but smile till now:
Now, good my lord, give me the scope of justice
My patience here is touch'd. I do perceive
These poor informal creatures are no more

But instruments of some more mightier member
That sets them on: let me have way, my lord,
To find this practise out.

Duke

                   Ay, with my heart.
You, Lord Escalus; lend her your kind pains
To find out this abuse, whence 'tis derived.
There is another friar that set them on;
Let him be sent for.

Thomas

Would he were here, my lord! For he indeed
Hath set these two here on to this complaint:
Your provost knows the place where he abides
And he may fetch him.

Duke (*to the* **Provost**)

Go do it instantly.
And you, the noble and well-warranted Isabel,
Do with your injuries as seems you best,
In any chastisement: I for a while will leave you;
But stir not you till you have well determined
Upon these slanderers.

Escalus

My lord, we'll do it throughly.

Exit **Duke**.

Call that same Angelo here once again; I would speak
with him.
Pray you, my lord, give me leave to question; you
shall see how I'll handle him.

Lucio

Not better than she, by his own report.

Escalus

Say you?

Lucio

    Marry, sir, I think, if you handled him privately,
    he would sooner confess: perchance, publicly,
    he'll be ashamed.

Escalus

    I will go darkly to work with him.

Re-enter **Justice**, **Angelo**, **Provost** *and* **Duke** *in his friar's habit.*

    Come hither, Angelo: here's a gentleman denies all that
    you have said.

Lucio

    My lord, here comes the rascal.

Escalus

    In very good time: speak not you to him till we call upon
    you.

Lucio

    Mum.

Escalus

    Come, sir: did you set these two on to slander this
    honourable judge?

Duke

    Where is the duke? 'tis he should hear me speak.

Escalus

    The duke's in us; and we will hear you speak:
    Look you speak justly.

Duke

               Is the duke gone?
    Then is your cause gone too. The duke's unjust.

Escalus

    Why thou irreverent friar, slander to the state.

Lucio

    This is the rascal; this is he I spoke of.

Isabel

What can you vouch against him, Signior Lucio?
Is this the man that you did tell us of?

Lucio

'Tis he, my indeed. Come hither: do you know me?

Duke

I remember you, sir, by the sound of your voice: I met
you at the prison, in the absence of the duke.

Lucio

O, did you so? And do you remember what you said of the
duke?

Duke

Most notedly, sir.

Lucio

Do you so, sir? And was the duke a fleshmonger, a fool,
and a coward, as you then reported him to be?

Duke

You must, sir, change persons with me, ere you make that
my report: you, indeed, spoke so of him; and much more,
much worse.

Lucio

O thou damnable fellow!

Duke

I protest I love the duke as I love myself.

Isabel

Hark, how the villain would close now, after his
treasonable abuses!

Escalus

Away with him to prison! Where is the provost?

Lucio

Come, sir; come, sir; come, sir; foh, sir!

Escalus

Away with you to prison.

Lucio

Why you, you lying rascal, you must be hooded, must
you? Show your knave's visage, with a pox to you! show
your sheep-biting face, and be hanged an hour! Will't not
off?

Pulls off the friar's hood, and discovers **Duke**.

This may prove worse than hanging.

Duke (*to* **Escalus**)

What you have spoke I pardon: sit you down:
We'll borrow place of him.
(*To* **Isabel**.) Now, by your leave.
Hast thou or word, or wit, or impudence,
That yet can do thee office? If thou hast,
Rely upon it till my tale be heard,
And hold no longer out.

Isabel

O my dread lord,
I should be guiltier than my guiltiness,
To think I can be undiscernible,
When I perceive your grace, like power divine,
Hath look'd upon my passes. Then, good prince,
No longer session hold upon my shame,
But let my trial be mine own confession:
Immediate sentence then and sequent death
Is all the grace I beg.

Duke

Come hither, Frederick.
Say, wast thou e'er contracted to this woman?

Frederick

I was, my lord.

Duke

Go take her hence, and marry her instantly.
Do you the office, friar; which consummate,
Return her here again. Go with him, provost.

Exeunt **Isabel**, **Frederick**, **Thomas** *and* **Provost**.

Escalus

My lord, I am more amazed at her dishonour
Than at the strangeness of it.

Duke

Come hither, Angelo.
Your friar is now your prince: as I was then.

Angelo

O, give me pardon,
That I, your vassal, have employ'd and pain'd
Your unknown sovereignty!

Duke

You are pardon'd, Angelo:
And now, dear youth, be you as free to us.
Your brother's death, I know, sits at your heart;
And you may marvel why I obscured myself,
Labouring to save his life. But, peace be with him!
That life is better life, past fearing death,
Than that which lives to fear: make it your comfort,
So happy is your brother.

Angelo

                    I do, my lord.

Re-enter **Isabel**, **Frederick**, **Thomas** *and* **Provost**.

Duke

For this new-married wife approaching here,
Whose salt imagination yet hath wrong'd
Your well defended honour, you must pardon
For Frederick's sake. But for your brother's life,
The very mercy of the law cries out
Most audible, even from his proper tongue,
'An Isabel for Claudio, death for death!'
Haste still pays haste, and leisure answers leisure;
Like doth quit like, and measure still for measure.
Then, Isabel, thy fault's thus manifested;

We do condemn thee to the very block
Where Claudio stoop'd to death, and with like haste.
Away with her!

Frederick

O my most gracious lord,
I hope you will not mock me with a wife.

Duke

I thought your marriage fit; for her possessions,
Although by confiscation they are ours,
We do instate and widow you withal,
To buy you a better match.

Frederick (*kneeling*)

O my dear lord,
I crave no other, nor no better wife.

Duke

Never crave her; we are definitive.

Frederick

O my good lord! Dear Angelo, take my part;
Lend me your knees, and all my life to come
I'll lend you all my life to do you service.

Duke

Against all sense you do importune him.

Frederick

Angelo,
Dear Angelo, do yet but kneel by me;
Hold up your hands, say nothing; I'll speak all.
O Angelo will you not lend a knee?

Duke

She dies for Claudio's death.

Angelo (*kneeling*)

Most bounteous sir, I partly think
A due sincerity govern'd her deeds,

Till she did look on me: since it is so,
Let her not die.

Duke

Stand up, I say.
I have bethought me of another fault.
Provost, how came it Claudio was beheaded
At an unusual hour?

Provost

It was commanded so.

Duke

Had you a special warrant for the deed?

Provost

No, my good lord; it was by private message.

Duke

For which I do discharge you of your office:
Give up your keys.

Provost

Pardon me, noble lord:
I thought it was a fault, but knew it not;
Yet did repent me, after more advice;
For testimony whereof, one in the prison,
That should by private order else have died,
I have reserved alive.

Duke

Go fetch him hither; let me look upon him.

Exit **Provost**.

Escalus

I am sorry, one so learned and so wise
Should slip so grossly, in the heat of blood.

Isabel

I am sorry that such sorrow I procure:
And so deep sticks it in my penitent heart
That I crave death more willingly than mercy.

Re-enter **Provost**, *with* **Claudio** *muffled.*

Provost

This is here a prisoner that I saved.
(*Unmuffles* **Claudio**.) As like almost to Claudio as himself.

Duke (*to* **Angelo**)

If he be like your brother, for his sake
Is he pardon'd; and, for your lovely sake,
Give me your hand and say you will be mine.
He is my brother too: but fitter time for that.
Well, Isabel, your evil quits you well:
I find an apt remission in myself;
And yet here's one in place I cannot pardon.
(*To* **Lucio**.) You, sirrah, wherein have I so deserved of
you?

Lucio

'Faith, my lord. If you will hang me for it, you may; but I
had rather it would please you I might be whipped.

Duke

Whipped first, sir, and hanged after.
Proclaim it, Justice, round about the city.
Is any woman wrong'd by this lewd fellow,
Whom he begot with child, let her appear,
And he shall marry her: the nuptial finish'd,
Let him be whipped and hang'd.

Lucio

Marrying a punk, my lord, is pressing to death,
whipping, and hanging.

Duke

Slandering a prince deserves it.
Upon mine honour, thou shalt marry her.
Thy slanders I forgive, and therewithal
Remit thy other forfeits.
She, Claudio, that you wrong'd, look you restore.
Joy to you, Frederick! Love him, Isabel.
Thanks, good friend Escalus, for thy much goodness:

There's more behind that is more gratulate.
Angelo, I have a motion much imports your good;
Whereto if you'll a willing ear incline,
What's mine is yours and what is yours is mine.

Exeunt.

For a complete listing of
Methuen Drama titles, visit:
www.bloomsbury.com/drama

Follow us on Twitter and keep up to date
with our news and publications
@MethuenDrama